2

FOCUS

ON

GRAMMAR

AN INTEGRATED SKILLS APPROACH

THIRD EDITION

SAMUELA ECKSTUT

PEARSON
Longman

FOCUS ON GRAMMAR 2: An Integrated Skills Approach
Workbook

Pearson Education, 10 Bank Street, White Plains, NY 10606

Staff credits: The people who made up the *Focus on Grammar 2 Workbook* team, representing
editorial, production, design, and manufacturing, are: Rhea Banker, Aerin Csigay, Christine
Edmonds, Nancy Flaggman, Ann France, Margo Gramer, Laura Le Dréan, and Laurie Neaman.
Cover images: (center) Alan Kearney/Getty Images, (middle) Nick Koudis/Getty Images, (background)
Comstock Images/Getty Images
Text composition: ElectraGraphics, Inc.
Text font: 11/13 Sabon, 10/13 Myriad Roman
Illustrators: Steve Attoe, p. 62; Chris Gash, pp. 58–59; Dave Sullivan, pp. 46, 126–127;
Gary Torrisi, p. 97.
Photo credit: David R. Frazier Photolibrary, Inc. p. 100.

About the Author

Samuela Eckstut has taught ESL and EFL for over twenty-five years, in the United States,
Greece, Italy, and England. Currently she is teaching at Boston University, Center for English
Language and Orientation Programs (CELOP). She has authored or co-authored numerous texts
for the teaching of English, notably *Strategic Reading 1, 2* and *3, What's in a Word? Reading and
Vocabulary Building; In the Real World; First Impressions; Beneath the Surface; Widely Read;* and
Finishing Touches.

ISBN: 0-13-189974-0 (Workbook)

LONGMAN ON THE **WEB**

Longman.com offers online resources for
teachers and students. Access our Companion
Websites, our online catalog, and our local
offices around the world.

Visit us at **longman.com.**

Printed in the United States of America
11 12 13 V031 13 12 11 10

Contents

The Present of *Be*: Statements

1 | AFFIRMATIVE AND NEGATIVE STATEMENTS WITH *BE*

Complete the sentences with **is**, **am**, *or* **are**.

1. David Beckham _____*is*_____ not from Brazil.

2. Ronaldo _____ a Brazilian soccer player.

3. I _____ not a famous soccer player.

4. Soccer _____ popular in England.

5. Baseball and volleyball _____ sports.

6. Baseball _____ not the number one sport in Brazil.

7. Baseball players _____ from different countries.

8. Baseball _____ not my favorite sport.

9. Nicole Kidman _____ not a soccer player.

10. I _____ a big soccer fan.

2 | SUBJECT PRONOUNS

Change the underlined words. Use **he, she, it, we,** *or* **they.**

    Hello. I am Rocco. My last name is Marciano. ~~My last name~~ *It* is an Italian name. My family
                                             1.
and I are from Italy. Now <u>my family and I</u> live here. Anna is my mother. <u>My mother</u> is from a
                 2.   **3.**
village in Abruzzi. <u>The village</u> is very small. Silvano is my father. <u>My father</u> is from Naples.
                4.   **5.**
<u>Naples</u> is a big city in the south of Italy. I am from Naples, too.
  6.

    My parents are in Italy now. <u>My parents</u> are on vacation. I am at home with my sisters.
                                        7.
<u>My sisters and I</u> are not happy alone. <u>My sisters</u> are always angry with me. My brother is
   8.   **9.**
lucky. <u>My brother</u> is not at home. <u>My brother</u> is at college. <u>The college</u> is far away.
       10.   **11.**   **12.**

3 | AFFIRMATIVE OF *BE*

*Write true statements. Use words from columns **A**, **B**, and **C** in each sentence.*

A	B	C	
I		at home	late
My best friend		at work	short
My mother	am	cold	tall
My father	is	friendly	thin
My teacher	are	happy	worried
My parents		heavy	a student
My classmates		hot	a nice person

1. <u>I am a student.</u>

2. _____

3. _____

4. _____

5. _____

6. _____

7. _____

8. _____

9. _____

10. _____

4 | NEGATIVE STATEMENTS WITH *BE*

*Make the following sentences true by using **not**. Then write another sentence with the correct information.*

1. Dallas is a state.

   <u>Dallas is not a state. It is a city.</u>

2. California is a country.

   _____

3. Russia is small.

   _____

4. Egypt and China are people.

   _____

5. Boston and New York are in Canada.

   _____

6. Florida is a city.

   _____

7. The sun is cold.

   _____

8. Toyotas and Fords are airplanes.

   _____

9. Ottawa is the capital of the United States.

   _____

10. Cigarettes are good for people.

    _____

11. The sun and the moon are near Earth.

    _____

5 | AFFIRMATIVE AND NEGATIVE STATEMENTS WITH *BE*

Complete the sentences. Use **is, is not, are,** *or* **are not.**

1. Apples _____ *are not* _____ black.

2. The Earth _____ round.

3. The sun _____ cold.

4. Ice cream and chocolate _____ good for you.

5. Lemons _____ yellow.

6. Cars _____ cheap.

7. Peter _____ a name.

8. An elephant _____ a small animal.

9. English, Spanish, and Arabic _____ languages.

10. The president of the United States _____ a doctor.

6 | CONTRACTIONS OF AFFIRMATIVE STATEMENTS WITH *BE*

Write the conversations in full form.

1. A: Mario's a good volleyball player.   *Mario is a good volleyball player.*

   B: Maria's good, too.   *Maria is good, too.*

2. A: We're from New York. _____

   B: I'm from New York, too. _____

3. A: I'm a big baseball fan. _____

   B: I'm not. _____

4. A: Jessica's a very good soccer player. _____

   B: She's a good student, too. _____

5. A: You're Mark, right? _____

   B: No, I'm not Mark. I'm his brother Mike. _____

6. A: Pedro's 19. _____

   B: No, he's not. He's 16. _____

7. A: Volleyball's a popular sport. Soccer's popular, too. _____

   _____

   B: They're not popular in my country. _____

7 | CONTRACTIONS OF AFFIRMATIVE AND NEGATIVE STATEMENTS WITH *BE*

Write the conversations with contractions.

1. A: Mario is a good volleyball player.   *Mario's a good volleyball player.*

   B: Maria is good, too.   *Maria's good, too.*

2. A: Yung-Hee and Ali are not in class today. _____

   B: They are at a game. _____

3. A: The teacher is not in class. _____

   B: I know. She is sick. _____

4. A: Antonio is a student in your class. _____

 B: His name is not on my list. _____

5. A: Melinda is a good singer. _____

 B: She is pretty too. _____

6. A: I am right. _____

 B: No, you are not. You are wrong. _____

7. A: They are my books. _____

 B: No, they are not. They are my books. _____

8 | EDITING

Correct the paragraph. There are seven mistakes. The first mistake is already corrected.

 My favorite sport ~~are~~ *is* baseball. It be popular in the United States. My favorite players are Pedro Martinez and Orlando Cabrera. Are baseball players in the United States. But they not from the United States. Pedro Martinez he is from the Dominican Republic. Orlando Cabrera is no from the Dominican Republic. He from Colombia.

2 The Present of *Be*: *Yes/No* Questions

1 | AFFIRMATIVE STATEMENTS AND *YES/NO* QUESTIONS WITH *BE*

Put a question mark **(?)** *at the end of each question. Put a period* **(.)** *at the end of each sentence.*

1. It is December 15th .

2. Is it December 15th ?

3. Are you hungry ___

4. Are you and your classmates unhappy ___

5. Is your teacher in school today ___

6. We are very good students ___

7. I am very thirsty ___

8. Is your watch expensive ___

9. Michigan is near Canada ___

10. Are the students from the same country ___

11. Is your car comfortable ___

12. This exercise is easy ___

2 | YES/NO QUESTIONS AND SHORT ANSWERS WITH *BE*

Match the questions and answers.

_d_	**1.** Is Preeda from Thailand?	**a.**	Yes, she is. She's in the kitchen with my father.
____	**2.** Are Pat and Tom American?	**b.**	Yes, we are. Our teacher's wonderful.
____	**3.** Are you Lucy Simone	**c.**	Yes, they're in the garden.
____	**4.** Are you ready?	**d.**	Yes, he is. He's from Bangkok.
____	**5.** Is the doctor in the office?	**e.**	No, we're students at Kennedy High School.
____	**6.** Are Mr. and Mrs. Saris here?	**f.**	No, they're not. They're British.
____	**7.** Is the TV in the living room?	**g.**	No, it isn't. It's in the bedroom.
____	**8.** Is John married?	**h.**	No, I'm Anna Sanchez.
____	**9.** Is the book good?	**i.**	Yes, it is. It's very interesting.
____	**10.** Are you students at King High School?	**j.**	No, I'm not. Please wait a minute.
____	**11.** Is your mother home?	**k.**	Yes, he is. His wife's a detective.
____	**12.** Are you and the other students happy in this class?	**l.**	Yes, she's with a patient.

3 | YES/NO QUESTIONS AND SHORT ANSWERS WITH *BE*

Write questions. Then answer them. Use short answers.

1. the teacher / you / Are

Are you the teacher? _____ _No, I'm not._ _____

2. you / Are / happy

_____ _____

3. a student / your mother / Is

_____ _____

4. today / Is / Thursday

_____ _____

5. Are / from California / your friends

_____ _____

(continued)

6. busy / your friend / Is

_____   _____

7. a singer / Are / you

_____   _____

8. your teacher / Is / friendly

_____   _____

9. your mother and father / Canadian / Are

_____   _____

10. Are / married / you

_____   _____

11. young / your classmates / Are

_____   _____

12. it / Is / 11 o'clock

_____   _____

4 | EDITING

Correct the conversation. There are seven mistakes. The first mistake is already corrected.

CLAUDIA: Excuse me. ~~This is~~ ^{Is this} Room 202?

TEACHER: Yes, it's.

ENRIQUE: Oh. We late for class?

TEACHER: You are yes.

ENRIQUE: We're very sorry.

TEACHER: That's OK. You are Ana Leite and Fernando Romeiro from Brazil?

CLAUDIA: No, we're are not. I'm Claudia Rodriguez. And this is Enrique Montero. We're from

Venezuela.

TEACHER: Hmm . . . your names are not on my list. Are you in English 4?

CLAUDIA: No, I don't think. I think we're in English 2.

TEACHER: Then this is not your class. You're in Room 302.

The Past of *Be*

1 | AFFIRMATIVE AND NEGATIVE STATEMENTS WITH THE PAST OF *BE*

Check (✓) the sentences that are true about your own life. Change the sentences that are wrong.

When I was seven years old, . . .

_____ 1. my favorite food was ice cream. _my favorite food was not ice cream._

__✓__ 2. I was not in the United States. _____

_____ 3. my parents were always busy. _____

_____ 4. I was good at sports. _____

_____ 5. my friends were seven too. _____

_____ 6. my friends and I were in the same class. _____

_____ 7. I was a good student. _____

_____ 8. my teacher was a man. _____

_____ 9. my home was in a big city. _____

_____ 10. my grandparents were alive. _____

2 | AFFIRMATIVE AND NEGATIVE STATEMENTS WITH THE PAST OF *BE*

*Write sentences. Use **was**, **wasn't**, **were**, or **weren't**.*

1. Abraham Lincoln / born / in England

   Abraham Lincoln wasn't born in England.

2. Picasso and Michelangelo / painters

   Picasso and Michelangelo were painters.

3. William Shakespeare and Charles Dickens / Canadian

   _____

(continued)

9

4. Bill Clinton / the first president of the United States

_____

5. Charlie Chaplin and Marilyn Monroe / movie stars

_____

6. The end of World War I / in 1942

_____

7. *Titanic* / the name of a movie

_____

8. Toronto and Washington, D.C. / big cities 300 years ago

_____

9. Indira Gandhi and Napoleon / famous people

_____

10. Nelson Mandela / a political leader

_____

11. Oregon and Hawaii / part of the United States / in 1776

_____

12. Disneyland / a famous place / 100 years ago

_____

3 | EDITING

Correct the mistake in each question. Then answer the questions. Use short answers.

     Was
1. ~~Were~~ your mother at home last night? _Yes, she was. (OR No, she wasn't.)_ _____

2. You were a student 10 years ago? _____

3. Are you in English class yesterday? _____

4. Was all the students in class last week? _____

5. Is the weather nice yesterday? _____

6. Your teacher was at work two days ago? _____

4 | THE PRESENT AND PAST OF *BE*

Complete the conversation. Use **is**, **are**, **was**, *or* **were**.

A: It _____is_____ a beautiful day.
1.

B: Yes, it is—especially because the weather _____was_____ so terrible yesterday. The weather in this
2.

city _____ so strange. One day it _____ warm, and the next day it _____ cold.
3.   4.   5.

A: You _____ right about that. In my country, it _____ always warm and sunny.
6.   7.

B: _____ it warm in the winter, too?
8.

A: Uh-huh. It _____ usually between 70 and 90 degrees. Last Christmas I _____ home
9.   10.

for two weeks, and it _____ sunny and warm. My friends and I _____ at the beach
11.   12.

every day. How about you? _____ you here this past Christmas?
13.

B: Yeah. My parents _____ here for five days for a visit. We _____ cold most of the
14.   15.

time, and my mother _____ ill for a few days. They _____ happy to see me, but they
16.   17.

_____ glad to leave this awful weather.
18.

A: _____ your parents back home now?
19.

B: No, they _____ on another vacation—this time, in a warm place.
20.

4 Count Nouns

1 | NOUNS

Match the people with their occupations.

_d_	**1.** Romario	**a.**	actor
____	**2.** Tom Cruise	**b.**	politician
____	**3.** Elizabeth II	**c.**	musician
____	**4.** Céline Dion	**d.**	athlete
____	**5.** Neil Armstrong	**e.**	queen
____	**6.** Yo Yo Ma	**f.**	astronaut
____	**7.** Hillary Clinton	**g.**	author
____	**8.** J. K. Rowling	**h.**	singer

2 | NOUNS WITH *A / AN*

Write sentences about the people in Exercise 1.

1. _Romario is an athlete._ _____

2. _____

3. _____

4. _____

5. _____

6. _____

7. _____

8. _____

3 | PLURAL NOUNS

Say these plural nouns. Then write them in the correct columns.

boxes	b̶o̶y̶s̶	c̶a̶r̶r̶o̶t̶s̶	classes	dictionaries
girls	h̶o̶s̶t̶e̶s̶s̶e̶s̶	houses	lemons	notebooks
roommates	sons	states	students	watches

/z/	/ɪz/	/s/
boys	hostesses	carrots
_____	_____	_____
_____	_____	_____
_____	_____	_____
_____	_____	_____

4 | PLURAL NOUNS

Complete the sentences. Use the plural form of the words in the box.

actor	city	country	mountain	river	state	watch
c̶a̶r̶	continent	man	province	song	university	w̶o̶m̶a̶n̶

1. Toyotas and Fords are _____ cars _____.

2. Mrs. Robb and Ms. Hernandez are _____ women _____.

3. Mr. Katz and John Mallin are _____.

4. "A Hard Day's Night" and "Happy Birthday to You" are _____.

5. London and Cairo are _____.

6. The Nile and the Amazon are _____.

7. Asia and Africa are _____.

8. Florida and Michigan are _____.

9. Brazil and Kenya are _____.

10. Ontario and Quebec are _____.

11. Harvard and Yale are _____.

12. Seikos and Rolexes are _____.

13. Nicole Kidman and Jennifer Lopez are _____.

14. The Himalayas and the Alps are _____.

5 | IRREGULAR PLURAL NOUNS

Write the singular or plural form of the nouns.

1.   4 women
   + 1   *woman*
      5   *women*

2.   1 child
   + 2 _____
      3 _____

3.   1 tooth
   + 6 _____
      7 _____

4.   3 feet
   + 1 _____
      4 _____

5.   6 grandchildren
   + 1 _____
      7 _____

6.   8 people
   + 1 _____
      9 _____

7.   1 sister-in-law
   + 2 _____
      3 _____

6 | SINGULAR AND PLURAL NOUNS

*Unscramble the words. Then write sentences with **it's** or **they're**. Add **a** or **an** where necessary.*

1. rac   *car*   *It's a car.*

2. wrofles   *flowers*   *They're flowers.*

3. thoscel _____ _____

4. shotop _____ _____

5. labelurm _____ _____

6. arseer _____ _____

7. pils _____ _____

8. drib _____ _____

9. hetet _____ _____

10. aht _____ _____

11. stanp _____ _____

12. reigran _____ _____

Descriptive Adjectives

1 | OPPOSITES OF ADJECTIVES

Write the opposites of the underlined words.

1. **A:** Is the village <u>clean</u>?

   B: Yes, but the beaches are _____*dirty*_____.

2. **A:** Is the exercise <u>easy</u>?

   B: Yes, but the next one is _____.

3. **A:** Is the book <u>interesting</u>?

   B: Yes, but the movie is _____.

4. **A:** Is Ann <u>friendly</u>?

   B: Yes, but her daughter is _____.

5. **A:** Is the Toyota <u>used</u>?

   B: Yes, but the Ford is _____.

6. **A:** Is the hotel <u>big</u>?

   B: Yes, but the rooms are _____.

7. **A:** Is the bed <u>comfortable</u>?

   B: Yes, but the chair is _____.

8. **A:** Are the paintings <u>beautiful</u>?

   B: Yes, but the photos are _____.

9. **A:** Are the women <u>young</u>?

   B: Yes, but the men are _____.

10. **A:** Are your feet <u>cold</u>?

    B: Yes, but my hands are _____.

2 | EDITING

Correct the mistake in each sentence. Then write correct sentences.

1. The olds shoes are over there.

   The old shoes are over there.

2. They are men honest.

   _____

3. They are talls girls.

   _____

4. They are animals intelligent.

   _____

5. Those books are expensives.

   _____

6. Eggs are whites or brown.

   _____

7. They are actors good.

   _____

8. These watches are cheaps.

   _____

9. They are stories interesting.

   _____

3 | ADJECTIVES AND NOUNS

Combine the two sentences into one sentence.

1. You are kind. You are people.

   You are kind people.

2. It is a movie. It is long.

   _____

3. The Prado is a museum. The Prado is famous.

   _____

4. You are a photographer. You are unusual.

   _____

5. They are buildings. They are interesting.

   _____

6. He is a man. He is intelligent.

   _____

7. It is a village. It is crowded.

   _____

8. She is a soccer player. She is popular.

   _____

9. We are students. We are good.

   _____

10. This is an exercise. This is easy.

    _____

6 Prepositions of Place

1 | PREPOSITIONS OF PLACE

Draw a picture of each sentence.

1. A cat is under a chair.

2. A dog is on a chair.

3. A ball is between a dog and a cat.

4. A man is next to a chair.

5. An apple is next to a banana.

6. A woman is behind a little girl.

7. A ball is under a car.

8. A bicycle is next to a house.

9. Some flowers are between two trees.

10. Two boxes are on a bed.

2 | PREPOSITIONS OF PLACE

Look at the map on page A-3 of your Student Book. Complete the sentences. Use **near**, **between**, **next to**, *or* **in**.

1. Seattle is _____*in*_____ Washington.

2. Saskatchewan is _____ Manitoba and Alberta.

3. Pennsylvania is _____ New Jersey.

4. Maine is _____ Massachusetts.

5. Halifax is _____ Nova Scotia.

6. Kansas is _____ Arkansas and Iowa.

7. Indiana is _____ Ohio and Illinois.

8. Prince Edward Island is _____ Canada.

9. Idaho is _____ Oregon.

10. Ottawa is _____ Montreal.

3 | PREPOSITIONS OF PLACE

*Complete the conversation. Use **in**, **on**, or **at**.*

A: Where's your home?

B: ___In___ Canada.
   1.

A: Where _____ Canada?
   2.

B: _____ Vancouver.
   3.

A: Where _____ Vancouver?
   4.

B: _____ Hastings Street.
   5.

A: Where _____ Hastings Street?
   6.

B: _____ 526 Hastings Street.
   7.

A: Is your apartment _____ the first floor or the second floor?
   8.

B: It's _____ the twenty-third floor.
   9.

A: Oh. So is your home _____ a big apartment building?
   10.

B: Very big.

Wh- Questions

1 | QUESTION WORDS

Write the correct question words. Use **who**, **what**, **why**, or **where**.

1. _____Who_____? My mother.

2. _____Where_____? At home.

3. _____? My best friend.

4. _____? Because she's tired.

5. _____? On Park Street.

6. _____? A sandwich.

7. _____? Because it's interesting.

8. _____? Brazil.

9. _____? Shakespeare.

10. _____? Soccer and basketball.

11. _____? Under the bed.

12. _____? A bird.

2 | *WH-* QUESTIONS AND ANSWERS WITH *BE*

Write questions. Then find an answer for each question from Exercise 1. Write the answer
next to the question.

1. were / parents / Where / your

   _Where were your parents?_____   _At home._____

2. in / is / car / the / Who

   _Who is in the car?_____   _My mother._____

3. What / you / good at / sports / are

   _____   _____

4. from / Where / they / are

   _____   _____

5. in / Who / your / the / garden / was / woman

   _____   _____

(continued)

6. in bed / your mother / Why / is

_____   _____

7. shoes / are / Where / my

_____   _____

8. bag / was / the / What / in

_____   _____

9. post office / the / is / Where

_____   _____

10. Who / your / writer / favorite / is

_____   _____

11. the class / Why / popular / is

_____   _____

12. tree / What / the / is / in

_____   _____

3 | QUESTION WORDS

Complete the sentences. Use **who**_,_ **what**_,_ **why**_, or_ **where**_._

DAD: _____*What*_____'s this?
        1.

LAURA: It's a painting.

DAD: I know that. _____'s it here in the kitchen?
                  2.

LAURA: I don't know. It's not my painting. It's Mike's painting.

DAD: _____'s your brother Mike?
      3.

LAURA: At the museum.

DAD: At the museum? Your brother? _____'s he at the museum?
                               4.

LAURA: Because his friend is there.

DAD: _____'s his friend's name?
      5.

LAURA: Ratana.

DAD: _____'s Ratana?
      6.

LAURA: Mike's girlfriend.

DAD: Mike's girlfriend?

LAURA: Uh-huh.

DAD: Ratana's an unusual name. _____'s she from?
7.

LAURA: Dad, I don't know. She's not my girlfriend.

4 | *WH-* QUESTIONS

Write the questions. Use **who**, **what**, **why**, *or* **where**.

1. **A:** _Who is he? (OR Who's he?)_____

   B: He's one of the students in my English class.

2. **A:** _____

   B: The hospital? It's on Porter Street.

3. **A:** _____

   B: John Wayne? He was an actor.

4. **A:** _____

   B: Room 203 . . . Room 203. I'm sorry. I don't know.

5. **A:** _____

   B: I think your keys are on the TV.

6. **A:** _____

   B: Nelson Mandela and Boris Yeltsin were leaders of their countries.

7. **A:** _____

   B: On the phone? It was a friend from school.

8. **A:** _____

   B: Cadillacs are cars.

9. **A:** _____

   B: It's my answering machine.

10. **A:** _____

    B: The wastepaper basket is next to the desk.

11. **A:** _____

    B: Last night? I was at home.

UNIT 8 The Simple Present: Affirmative and Negative Statements

1 | AFFIRMATIVE STATEMENTS WITH THE SIMPLE PRESENT

Read the job descriptions. Answer the questions. Use the words in the box.

cook	flight attendant	pilot	salesperson
doctor	~~mechanic~~	professor	secretary

1. Daniel fixes cars. He works in a garage. What is he?

   He's a mechanic.

2. Dina and Lesley answer telephones and type letters. They work in a college office. What are they?

   _____

3. Captain Phillips goes to the airport every day. He flies airplanes. What is he?

   _____

4. Kay Williams gives lectures and meets with students. She works in a university. What is she?

   _____

5. Ben and Rachel work on an airplane. They serve meals and drinks to passengers. What are they?

   _____

6. I work in a restaurant. I prepare the food. What am I?

   _____

7. I work in a store. I sell refrigerators. What am I?

   _____

8. Ellen helps sick people. She works in a hospital. What is she?

   _____

2 │ AFFIRMATIVE AND NEGATIVE STATEMENTS WITH THE SIMPLE PRESENT

Complete each sentence with the correct verb. Use the simple present form.

1. Mary is a taxi driver. She _____*drives*_____ a taxi.

2. Stuart is a Spanish teacher. He _____ Spanish.

3. Maria Domingo is a singer. She _____.

4. Nassos Morona is a dancer. He _____.

5. Bill Bright is a baseball player. He _____ baseball.

6. Shirley Simpson is a bank manager. She _____ a bank.

7. Sam and Victor are trash collectors. They _____ trash.

8. Margaret and Phil are house painters. They _____ houses.

9. Lou is a window washer. He _____ windows.

10. Oscar, Tom, and Steve are firefighters. They _____ fires.

3 │ AFFIRMATIVE AND NEGATIVE STATEMENTS WITH THE SIMPLE PRESENT

Complete the conversation. Use the correct form of the verbs in parentheses.

A: Tell me about you and your family.

B: My husband and I _____*are*_____ pretty traditional. I _____ care of the
  1. (be)   **2. (take)**

  home, and he _____ to work. He _____ a business in town, but
                    3. (go)   **4. (have)**

  we _____ in an old house in the country.
       5. (live)

A: Alone?

B: Oh, no. We _____ alone. We _____ eight children—seven boys
                6. (not live)   **7. (have)**

  and one girl. Two of them _____ with us anymore. Our daughter
                                8. (not live)

  _____ married, and she _____ with her family. She
       9. (be)   **10. (live)**

  _____ two children. One of our sons _____ also married, but he
       11. (have)   **12. (be)**

  _____ any children. Our other six sons _____ with us. One of
       13. (not have)   **14. (live)**

  (continued)

them, Marvin, _____ at the local college and _____ part-time.

15. (study)   16. (work)

He _____ home every morning at around six o'clock and _____

17. (leave)   18. (not come)

home until seven or eight in the evening. It _____ a good schedule at all. Our

19. (not be)

son Russell _____ my husband, and the other boys _____ to high

20. (help)   21. (go)

school.

A: Are you busy all the time?

B: Oh, yes. I _____ much free time at all. That's why we _____ to

22. (not have)   23. (try)

rest on Sundays. We _____ up until nine o'clock.

24. (not get)

4 | AFFIRMATIVE AND NEGATIVE STATEMENTS WITH THE SIMPLE PRESENT

Correct the sentences. Use words from the box.

a big population	grass	the sun
during the day	mice	0° C
~~in the east~~	Antarctic	100° C
a hot climate	sand	big ears

1. The sun rises in the west.

   The sun doesn't rise in the west. It rises in the east. _____

2. Water boils at 90° C.

   _____

3. Water freezes at 5° C.

   _____

4. The sun goes around the Earth.

   _____

5. Penguins come from the Arctic.

   _____

6. Cows eat meat.

   _____

7. China has a small population.

_____

8. Deserts have a lot of water.

_____

9. Elephants have small ears.

_____

10. Egypt has a cold climate.

_____

11. The sun shines at night.

_____

12. Cats run after dogs.

_____

9 The Simple Present: *Yes/No* Questions and Short Answers

1 | *YES / NO* QUESTIONS WITH THE SIMPLE PRESENT

Write the questions in the correct boxes.

1. Do you feel a pain here?
2. Do you know how to type?
3. Do you want a plastic bag or a paper bag?
4. Do you have any experience?
5. Do you want a one-bedroom or a two-bedroom apartment?
6. Do you get many headaches?
7. Do you have any other fresh fish?
8. Do you speak a foreign language?
9. Do you want a place near the center of town?
10. Does your back hurt?
11. Does this orange juice cost $2.50?
12. Does the house have two bathrooms?

PEOPLE OFTEN ASK THIS AT . . .

A. a job interview	**B.** a doctor's office
	Do you feel a pain here?
C. a real estate office	**D.** a supermarket

2 | YES / NO QUESTIONS AND SHORT ANSWERS WITH THE SIMPLE PRESENT

Match the questions and answers.

_e_ 1. Does the sun go around the Earth?

_____ 2. Do banks have money?

_____ 3. Do you speak English perfectly?

_____ 4. Does Peru have many mountains?

_____ 5. Do supermarkets sell cars?

_____ 6. Does the president of the United States live on the moon?

_____ 7. Does the president of the United States live in the White House?

_____ 8. Do you eat every day?

a. Yes, it does.

b. No, they don't.

c. No, I don't.

d. Yes, I do.

e. No, it doesn't.

f. Yes, they do.

g. No, he doesn't.

h. Yes, he does.

3 | YES / NO QUESTIONS AND SHORT ANSWERS WITH THE SIMPLE PRESENT

Answer the questions. Use short answers.

	MICHAEL	**MARY**	**KAREN**	**LARRY**
Like rock music	✓	X	X	X
Watch TV every day	X	✓	X	✓
Wake up early	X	✓	X	✓
Go to bed late	X	✓	X	X
Study at night	✓	X	X	✓
✓ = Yes X = No				

1. Does Michael like rock music? _Yes, he does._

2. Do Karen and Larry go to bed late? _No, they don't._

3. Does Mary wake up early? _____

4. Does Karen study at night? _____

5. Do Michael and Larry study at night? _____

6. Does Mary watch TV every day? _____

7. Do Karen and Michael watch TV every day? _____

8. Does Larry go to bed late? _____

9. Do Mary and Larry wake up early? _____

10. Do Karen and Larry like rock music? _____

4 | NEGATIVE STATEMENTS WITH THE SIMPLE PRESENT

*Complete the sentences. Use **don't** or **doesn't**.*

1. Bell Mall has a music store, but Northshore Mall _____*doesn't*_____.

2. I go shopping a lot, but my friends _____*don't*_____.

3. My son wears a tie to work, but my husband _____.

4. Katie has a lot of jewelry, but her sister _____.

5. Ellen and Dave spend a lot of money on clothes, but Bea and Ken _____.

6. My friend buys used clothes, but I _____.

7. Yoko polishes her nails, but her roommates _____.

8. These shoes cost over $100, but the shoes over there _____.

9. My mother likes shopping, but I _____.

10. My classmates and I wear fashionable clothes, but our teacher _____.

5 | EDITING

Correct the mistake in each sentence.

    Do you
1. ~~You~~ need any help?

2. Does your roommate likes your girlfriend?

3. The teacher wear glasses?

4. Do Mr. Flagg have a car?

5. Does Jack and Jill sleep until ten o'clock?

6. Peter eat fast?

7. Are she leave for work at the same time every day?

8. Is the dog eat two times a day?

9. Does the doctor has your telephone number?

10. Football players play in the summer?

6 | *YES / NO* QUESTIONS WITH THE SIMPLE PRESENT

Complete the questions.

1. People do not come here on Sundays.

   _Do they come_____ on Saturdays?

2. Carlos has class on Mondays and Wednesdays.

   _____ class on Tuesdays, too?

3. The children like bananas.

   _____ apples, too?

4. We live in a house.

   _____ in a big house?

5. My boyfriend knows my brother.

   _____ your sister?

6. My wife and I want a hotel room.

   _____ a room for one or two nights?

7. I have two sisters.

   _____ any brothers?

8. Ms. Winchester doesn't wear glasses.

   _____ contact lenses?

9. My classmates and I do not like grammar exercises.

   _____ vocabulary exercises?

10. I do not know the answer to the first question.

    _____ the answer to the second question?

11. The saleswomen do not work in the afternoon.

    _____ in the morning?

12. That young man does not come from the United States.

    _____ from Canada?

10 The Simple Present: *Wh-* Questions

1 | QUESTION WORDS

Write the correct question words. Use **who, what, where, when, how,** *or* **why.**

1. _____What_____ ?   Cereal.

2. _____Why_____ ?   Because I'm tired.

3. _____ ?   At City Central Bank.

4. _____ ?   A suit and tie.

5. _____ ?   My teacher.

6. _____ ?   At noon.

7. _____ ?   His friends.

8. _____ ?   At his school.

9. _____ ?   In the morning.

10. _____ ?   Because I want to buy a sweatshirt.

11. _____ ?   Great.

12. _____ ?   In August.

2 | *WH-* QUESTIONS WITH THE SIMPLE PRESENT

Write questions. Then find an answer for each question in Exercise 1. Write the answers below.

1. want / to leave / do / Why / you

   _Why do you want to leave_____ ?   _Because I'm tired._____

2. for breakfast / What / you / have / do

   _____ ?   _____

3. feel / after / do / a nap / How / you

   _____ ?   _____

4. your / corrects / homework / Who

   _____ ?   _____

5. does / work / Rosita / Where

   _____ ?   _____

6. on vacation / When / go / you and your family / do

   _____ ?   _____

7. What / to work / wear / you / do

   _____ ?   _____

8. need / do / more money / you / Why

   _____ ?   _____

9. the / What time / eat / kids / do / lunch

   _____ ?   _____

10. come / the / mail / does / When

    _____ ?   _____

11. Doug / soccer / play / Where / does

    _____ ?   _____

12. visit / does / on Sundays / Mark / Who

    _____ ?   _____

3 | QUESTION WORDS

Complete the sentences. Use **who, what, where, when, how,** *or* **why.**

ROB: _____Who_____ gets up early?
1.

NAN: My husband does. He gets up at 4:00 A.M.

ROB: _____ does he get up?
2.

NAN: He sets his alarm clock.

ROB: _____ does he get up so early?
3.

NAN: He starts work at 5:30.

ROB: _____ does he do?
4.

NAN: He's a chef.

ROB: _____ does he work?
5.

NAN: He works downtown. He has his own restaurant.

ROB: _____ does the restaurant open?
6.

NAN: At seven o'clock.

ROB: Then _____ does he go to work so early?
7.

NAN: He has to open the door. The other workers come at 5:30, too.

ROB: And _____ do you do in the morning?
8.

NAN: I sleep.

4 | *WH-* QUESTIONS WITH THE SIMPLE PRESENT

Write the questions. Use **who**, **what**, **where**, **when**, **how**, *or* **why**.

1. *How do you feel after work?*

   I feel tired.

2. _____

   I drink tea at night because it helps me sleep.

3. _____

   I don't remember a lot about my dream, but it was scary.

4. _____

   In the morning? My roommate looks terrible.

5. _____

   Teenagers sleep late because they need a lot of sleep.

6. _____

   My roommate? She sleeps in the living room.

7. _____

   My mother usually wakes me up, but sometimes my father does.

8. _____

   We sleep late only on the weekends.

9. _____

   In the small bedroom? My little sister sleeps there.

10. _____

    After my nap? I exercise.

11. _____

    In my family? My brother sleeps a lot.

12. _____

    She wants to wake up her son.

UNIT

When, What + Noun;
Prepositions of Time;
Ordinal Numbers

1 | PREPOSITIONS OF TIME

Write the words in the correct columns.

~~4:00~~	May	the morning
March 20, 2006	~~Wednesday~~	the spring
night	Thursday	~~December~~
the evening	half past six	1888
June 30th	December 3rd	the summer

At	In	On
4:00	December	Wednesday

2 | PREPOSITIONS OF TIME

Celia doesn't have her appointment book. It's at your house. She calls you on February 2nd.
Look at her appointment book and answer her questions. Use **at**, **in**, *or* **on***.*

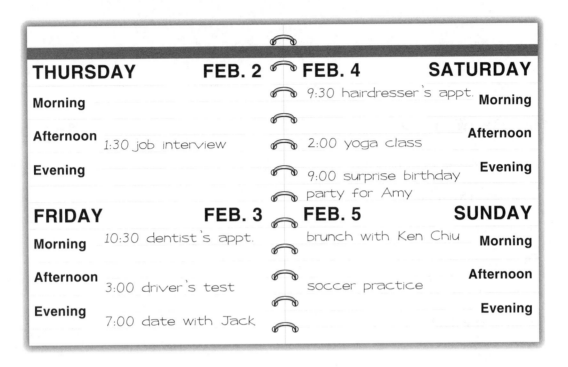

THURSDAY   FEB. 2   FEB. 4   SATURDAY

Morning   9:30 hairdresser's appt. **Morning**

Afternoon   1:30 job interview   2:00 yoga class   **Afternoon**

Evening   9:00 surprise birthday party for Amy   **Evening**

FRIDAY   FEB. 3   FEB. 5   SUNDAY

Morning   10:30 dentist's appt.   brunch with Ken Chiu   **Morning**

Afternoon   3:00 driver's test   soccer practice   **Afternoon**

Evening   7:00 date with Jack   **Evening**

1. When is my hairdresser's appointment on Saturday morning?

   It's at 9:30. _____

2. What time this afternoon is my job interview?

   _____

3. And when is my dentist's appointment tomorrow?

   _____

4. When's my brunch with Ken Chiu?

   _____

5. I know Amy's birthday party is this week, but when is it?

   _____

6. Is my yoga class at 2:00 or 3:00 on Saturday?

   _____

(continued)

7. What time is my date with Jack tomorrow?

   _____

8. I know I have soccer practice on Sunday? Is it in the morning?

   _____

9. What about my driver's test tomorrow? When's that?

   _____

3 | *WH-* QUESTIONS

Laura is always confused. Write questions.

1. **A:** Is lunch at two o'clock?

   B: No, it isn't.

   A: Then _what time is lunch?_ _____

   B: It's at twelve o'clock.

2. **A:** Is today Monday?

   B: No, it isn't.

   A: Then _what day is it?_ _____

   B: It's Sunday.

3. **A:** Is today June 10th?

   B: No, it isn't.

   A: Then _____

   B: It's June 11th.

4. **A:** Is it 10:30?

   B: No, it isn't.

   A: Then _____

   B: It's 11:30.

5. **A:** Is the meeting today?

   B: No, it isn't.

   A: Then _____

   B: It's tomorrow.

6. **A:** Is the meeting in the afternoon?

   B: No, it isn't.

   A: Then _____

   B: It's in the evening.

7. **A:** The meeting's at six o'clock, isn't it?

   B: No, it isn't.

   A: Then _____

   B: It's at 7:30.

8. **A:** I need some money. Is the bank open on Saturday?

   B: No, it isn't.

   A: Then _____

   B: It's open on Monday, Tuesday, Wednesday, Thursday, and Friday.

9. **A:** Is today your birthday?

   B: No, it isn't.

   A: Then _____

   B: It's tomorrow.

4 | ORDINAL NUMBERS

Write the numbers.

1. sixth _____6th_____
2. forty-fourth _____44th_____
3. ninth _____
4. twelfth _____
5. twenty-third _____
6. fifty-first _____
7. seventy-second _____
8. eightieth _____
9. ninety-fifth _____
10. one hundred and first _____
11. one hundred and sixteenth _____
12. two hundredth _____

5 | ORDINAL NUMBERS

Write the words for the numbers.

1. 4th _____fourth_____
2. 38th _____thirty-eighth_____
3. 3rd _____
4. 11th _____
5. 15th _____
6. 20th _____

7. 31st _____
8. 47th _____
9. 66th _____
10. 82nd _____
11. 99th _____
12. 103rd _____

6 | ORDINAL NUMBERS

Write the street names.

1. *Third Avenue and Thirty-second Street* _____
2. _____
3. _____
4. _____
5. _____
6. _____
7. _____

1.

2.

3.

4.

5.

6.

7.

7 | ORDINAL NUMBERS AND PREPOSITIONS OF TIME

When are the birthdays of Tony's friends and relatives? Write the dates.

APRIL

SUNDAY	MONDAY	TUESDAY	WEDNESDAY	THURSDAY	FRIDAY	SATURDAY
		1 Uncle Norman	2 Dad	3	4	5
6	7	8	9	10	11	12
13	14	15 Grandpa	16	17	18	19
20 Mom	21	22	23	24	25 Katie	26
27	28	29	30			

MAY

SUNDAY	MONDAY	TUESDAY	WEDNESDAY	THURSDAY	FRIDAY	SATURDAY
				1	2 Aunt Leona	3
4	5	6	7	8	9	10
11 Nick	12	13	14	15	16	17
18	19	20	21	22	23 Hanna	24
25	26	27	28 Adam	29	30 Elisa	31

1. When is his father's birthday? It's on April second.

2. When is Hanna's birthday? _____

3. When is Aunt Leona's birthday? _____

4. When is Uncle Norman's birthday? _____

5. When is Elisa's birthday? _____

6. When is his grandfather's birthday? _____

7. When is Katie's birthday? _____

8. When is Nick's birthday? _____

9. When is Adam's birthday? _____

10. When is his mother's birthday? _____

12 Possessive Nouns and Possessive Adjectives; Questions with *Whose*

1 | POSSESSIVE ADJECTIVES

Match the questions and answers.

___c___ 1. Is John your son?

_____ 2. Is your home on this street?

_____ 3. Is he Joe and Karen's son?

_____ 4. Is Ms. Turner's home near here?

_____ 5. Is she a famous actress?

_____ 6. Are they rich?

_____ 7. Is Martin Wong a doctor?

_____ 8. Is that man your friend?

_____ 9. Is our table ready?

a. No, their son is in another state.

b. No, but her office is.

c. No, Mark is my son.

d. No, it isn't. Please wait a minute.

e. No, we live in Los Angeles.

f. No, her sister is.

g. Yes, his office is near the hospital.

h. Yes, his name is Sam Miller.

i. No, but their friends are.

2 | POSSESSIVE ADJECTIVES

Complete the conversations. Use **my, your, his, her, our,** *or* **their.**

1. JACK: Is that my car?

   JILL: No, _____*your*_____ car isn't here.

2. BOB: Jim, is this _____ bag?

   JIM: No, it isn't. Maybe it's Sue and Harry's bag.

   BOB: No, _____ bag is over there.

3. **Mr. Wolf:** Is this Mrs. Waller's box?

   Barbara: No, that's not _____ box.

   Mr. Wolf: Is it Mr. Luca's box?

   Barbara: Maybe it's _____ box. I'm not sure.

4. **Mrs. Yu:** Is this your family's dog?

   Ben: No, _____ dog is black.

   Mrs. Yu: Is it Mr. and Mrs. Haley's dog?

   Ben: No, _____ dog is white.

5. **Alan:** Is this your office?

   Ron: No, _____ office is on the second floor.

   Alan: Is it Norma's office?

   Ron: No, _____ office is on the first floor.

6. **Becky:** Stella, is that _____ husband with you in the picture?

   Stella: Yes, _____ name is Dave.

   Becky: And who's this?

   Stella: It's _____ daughter. _____ name is Marie.

3 | POSSESSIVE ADJECTIVES AND SUBJECT PRONOUNS

Complete the sentences. Use subject pronouns or possessive adjectives.

1. Hi. I'm Claudia. ____*I*____'m from Colombia. ___*My*___ home is in Bogotá.

2. This is Henry. _____'s in Chicago. _____ apartment is always neat and clean.

3. This is Lisa. _____'s in New Jersey. Claudia is _____ roommate.

4. This is Tom, and this is Joanna. _____'re married. _____ last name is Kavalas. This is

   _____ home. _____'s beautiful.

5. Hello. I'm Joe and this is Bill. _____'re friends. _____ homes are in Arizona.

6. Hi. I'm Bruce. _____'m not married, but _____'m engaged. _____ fiancée is from

   Russia.

(continued)

7. This is Angela Woods. _____'s an accountant. _____ office is on Franklin Street.

8. My wife and I are happy to meet you. _____'re here on business. _____ hotel is near

   here. _____ name is the Park Hotel. _____'s a very nice place, but _____'s

   expensive.

9. These are our children. _____ names are Jill and Paul. _____'re not at home this

   month. _____'re with my in-laws.

4 | POSSESSIVE NOUNS, POSSESSIVE ADJECTIVES, AND SUBJECT PRONOUNS

Rewrite the sentences. Change the underlined words.

1. <u>Mark Gold's</u> an engineer.

   He's an engineer.

2. <u>Mark Gold's</u> wife's a dentist.

   His wife's a dentist.

3. Mariana's <u>Mr. and Mrs. Gold's</u> neighbor.

   _____

4. <u>Mariana's</u> last name is Martinez.

   _____

5. <u>Mariana's</u> an aunt.

   _____

6. Danny and Federico are <u>Mariana's</u> nephews.

   _____

7. <u>Danny's</u> eight years old.

_____

8. <u>Frederico's</u> eyes are blue.

_____

9. <u>Mariana's</u> dogs are always outside.

_____

10. <u>Danny's</u> afraid of the dogs.

_____

11. <u>The boys</u> were with their aunt yesterday.

_____

12. <u>Mariana</u> was with her dogs.

_____

13. <u>The dogs'</u> food was in the garage.

_____

14. <u>The dogs</u> were in the garage.

_____

15. <u>The children's</u> friends were not with them yesterday.

_____

16. <u>The children</u> were happy to be with their aunt.

_____

5 | QUESTIONS WITH *WHOSE*

Larry is at the supermarket. He has the wrong bag of food. Write questions. Use **whose**.

1. This is not my coffee.

   Whose coffee is this?

2. These are not my apples.

   Whose apples are these?

3. These are not my eggs.

   _____

4. These are not my bananas.

   _____

5. This is not my bread.

   _____

6. These are not my potatoes.

   _____

7. This is not my cake.

   _____

8. This is not my milk.

   _____

9. This is not my orange juice.

   _____

10. These are not my potato chips.

   _____

11. These are not my carrots.

   _____

12. This is not my bag.

   _____

6 | EDITING

Correct the sentences. Add ' or 's where necessary.

1. **A:** Is this Steve's report?

   B: I don't think so.

2. **A:** What are your daughters' names?

   B: Michele and Kathy.

3. **A:** What's Ms. Baker first name?

   B: It's Sandra.

4. **A:** Where's the men room?

   B: It's over there.

5. **A:** Is that your husband brother?

   B: No, that's my brother.

6. **A:** Where are the babies mothers?

   B: In the other room.

7. **A:** Is your school for girls and boys?

   B: No, it's a girls school.

8. **A:** Are your brothers wives friendly?

   B: One is.

9. **A:** Is that your son car?

   B: No, it isn't.

10. **A:** Where's the doctor office?

    B: It's on Cambridge Avenue.

11. **A:** A teacher job is difficult.

    B: I know.

12. **A:** I can't find my teacher.

    B: Look in the teachers lunchroom. Many teachers are in there.

7 | POSSESSIVE NOUNS

Look at the pictures. Complete the sentences.

1. The wallet is _____ *Al Green's* _____ .

2. The handbag is _____ .

3. The car is _____ .

4. The sweatshirt is _____ .

5. The notebook is _____ .

6. The jeans are _____ .

7. The desk is _____ .

8. The composition is _____ .

9. The shoes are _____ .

This / That / These / Those; Questions with *Or*

1 | THIS AND *THESE*

Complete the conversations. Use **this** *or* **these** *and* **is** *or* **are***.*

1. **A:** ___These___ ___are___ my gloves.

   B: No, they're not. ___These___ ___are___ your gloves and

   ___this___ ___is___ your hat.

2. **A:** _____ _____ a gift for you.

   B: Oh, thank you.

3. **A:** _____ cake _____ delicious.

   B: _____ cookies _____ good, too.

4. **A:** _____ table _____ expensive.

   B: _____ chairs _____ expensive, too.

5. **A:** Dana, _____ _____ Eric.

   B: Hi, Eric. It's nice to meet you.

6. **A:** _____ earrings _____ only $25.

   B: Really?

7. **A:** _____ _____ a boring party.

   B: You're right.

8. **A:** _____ _____ cool sneakers.

   B: _____ T-shirt _____ cool, too.

9. **A:** _____ flowers _____ for you.

   B: Thank you so much. They're beautiful

10. **A:** _____ _____ my parents in the photo.

    B: Really? They're so young.

2 | QUESTIONS WITH *THIS* AND *THESE*

Write questions. Use **What's this?** *or* **What are these?**

1. **A:** _What are these?_

   B: They're trees.

2. **A:** _____

   B: It's the sun.

3. **A:** _____

   B: It's my dog.

4. **A:** _____

   B: It's a car.

5. **A:** _____

   B: They're my dolls.

6. **A:** _____

   B: They're flowers.

7. **A:** _____

   B: It's a chair.

8. **A:** _____

   B: They're balls.

9. **A:** _____

   B: They're birds.

10. **A:** _____

    B: It's a house.

3 | *THAT* AND *THOSE*

Complete the conversation. Use **that** *or* **those**.

A: Are you enjoying the party?

B: Yes, very much. But I don't know a lot of the people. Who's _____that_____ handsome
    1.

guy over there?

A: Do you mean the guy next to _____ bookshelf?
          2.

B: No, the guy between _____ paintings on the wall.
         3.

A: He's my cousin, Dennis.

B: And _____ two people?
          4.

A: Which people?

B: _____ people in the corner.
       5.

A: They're also my cousins.

B: Don't tell me _____ woman on the sofa is also your cousin.
              6.

A: No, _____'s my Aunt Phyllis.
         7.

B: And is _____ man next to her her husband?
           8.

A: No, _____'s her brother, my Uncle Norman.
         9.

B: What about _____ kids in the bedroom?
             10.

A: Some of them are cousins, but _____ two at the door are my sisters.
                   11.

B: You have a big family. Are _____ nice-looking women near the kitchen your
               12.

relatives, too?

A: No, the one with the blond hair is my girlfriend, but I don't know the other woman.

4 | *THIS, THAT, THESE,* AND *THOSE*

*Complete the sentences. Use **this, that, these**, or **those**.*

1. Robert and his wife are sitting in their new car. Robert says, "I like _____*this*_____ car."

2. Doris looks out the window and sees someone. She doesn't know the person. Doris says,

   "Who's _____?"

3. A friend has a gift for Ted and puts a small box in his hand. Ted says, "What's

   _____?"

4. Sylvia and Elizabeth are at a party. Sylvia says to Elizabeth, "Isn't _____ a great

   party?"

5. Vicky and Peggy are looking in the window of a shoe store. Vicky says to Peggy, "Aren't

   _____ shoes beautiful?"

6. Vicky and Peggy are in the store now. Vicky has the shoes in her hands. Vicky says,

   "_____ shoes really are beautiful."

7. Mr. Graham comes into his office. He asks his secretary about some people in the waiting

   room. Mr. Graham says, "Are _____ people waiting for me?"

8. Richard and Sandy are looking for their car in the parking lot. Richard finally sees it. It's

   behind four other cars. Richard says, "_____'s our car. Do you see it?"

9. Frank is at the kitchen table. There's a dish of potatoes in front of him. Frank says to his

   brother, "_____ are my potatoes. Don't eat them."

10. Mr. and Mrs. Moreno are in their car. They're lost. Mr. Moreno sees a sign about 50 meters

    away. He asks his wife, "What does _____ sign say?"

5 | QUESTIONS WITH *OR*

Write questions with **or**.

1. *Do you like basketball or soccer?* _____

   I don't like soccer. I like basketball.

2. _____

   Vicente isn't Mexican. He's Brazilian.

3. _____

   It's not December 6th. It's December 5th.

4. _____

   The train doesn't arrive at 6:30. It arrives at 7:30.

5. _____

   I don't have a suitcase. I have a backpack.

6. _____

   Denver isn't in the East. It's in the West.

7. _____

   The guide doesn't speak French. She speaks Spanish.

8. _____

   The people don't leave on Monday. They leave on Sunday.

9. _____

   My bag isn't black. It's brown.

10. _____

    You don't need a coat. You need a sweater.

14 One / Ones / It

1 | ONE AND ONES

Match the sentences and responses.

<u>d</u> 1. Do you want the big box?

_____ 2. I like the black pants.

_____ 3. Is this towel for me?

_____ 4. I like the sneakers.

_____ 5. Please give me that eraser.

_____ 6. Which shoes do you like?

_____ 7. Are there any movie theaters near here?

_____ 8. Do you want the raisin cookies?

a. No, it's dirty. Take this one.

b. Which one?

c. The brown ones.

d. No, give me the small one.

e. No, I want the chocolate ones.

f. Yes, there's one on Broadway.

g. I don't. I like the gray ones.

h. Which ones?

2 | ONE AND ONES

Rewrite the questions with **one** *or* **ones**.

1. A: He doesn't like the black shoes.

   B: Which shoes does he like? ___*Which ones does he like?*___

2. A: I don't want the leather bag.

   B: Which bag do you want? _____

3. A: I don't like that picture.

   B: Do you like this picture? _____

4. A: This sweatshirt isn't on sale.

   B: Which sweatshirt is on sale? _____

5. A: Sarah doesn't have this CD.

   B: Which CDs does she have? _____

6. **A:** These socks are for girls.

   B: Which socks are for boys? _____

7. **A:** The blue scarf is from Italy.

   B: Is the red scarf from Italy, too? _____

8. **A:** The gold earrings are expensive.

   B: Are the silver earrings expensive, too? _____

3 | ONE, ONES, AND IT

Add **one**, **ones**, *or* **it** *where necessary.*

1. **A:** Which is your car?

   B: The blue.^one^

2. **A:** Do you want the black shoes?

   B: No, I prefer the brown.

3. **A:** Please bring that chair over here.

   B: The in the corner?

   A: Yes, please.

4. **A:** Do you need all the eggs?

   B: No, only the in the bowl.

5. **A:** This apple is good.

   B: You're lucky. This is terrible.

6. **A:** Is there a supermarket near here?

   B: No, but there's about a mile away.

7. **A:** Which pills do you want?

   B: The on the kitchen table.

8. **A:** Do you want a hamburger?

   B: No, but Carla wants.

9. **A:** I like the new Rockets CD.

   B: Yeah. I like, too.

10. **A:** These cherries are good.

    B: The other are better.

11. **A:** Do you want these sandwiches?

    B: No, give me the over there.

12. **A:** I like this apartment.

    B: But the on Fifth Street costs less.

13. **A:** My gray socks aren't clean.

    B: Here are your black.

14. **A:** Where's my cell phone?

    B: Is on the table near the door.

UNIT

15 The Present Progressive: Affirmative and Negative Statements

1 | AFFIRMATIVE STATEMENTS WITH THE PRESENT PROGRESSIVE

Match the sentences.

_d_ 1. Lou's at the supermarket.

_____ 2. Paul's at the ATM.

_____ 3. Linda's in the library.

_____ 4. The football players are on the field.

_____ 5. Doug's at the shopping mall.

_____ 6. Dr. Miller is in her office.

_____ 7. Susan's in the bathroom.

_____ 8. Thompson and her family are in the dining room.

_____ 9. Sharon and her boyfriend are at the beach.

_____ 10. Pete's at the office.

a. They're playing football.

b. She's studying.

c. She's examining a patient.

d. He's buying groceries.

e. He's getting some money.

f. They're eating dinner.

g. She's taking a shower.

h. They're lying in the sun.

i. He's writing a report.

j. He's buying a shirt.

2 | BASE FORM OF VERB + *ING*

Write the missing form of each verb.

Base Form	Base Form + -*ing*
1. have	_____having_____
2. _____sit_____	sitting
3. smile	_____
4. shine	_____
5. _____	raining

6. _____ making

7. sleep _____

8. listen _____

9. _____ running

10. hold _____

11. _____ talking

12. smoke _____

13. do _____

14. _____ putting

15. _____ beginning

16. read _____

17. _____ crying

18. stay _____

3 | PRESENT PROGRESSIVE STATEMENTS *RIGHT NOW* AND *THESE DAYS*

Write **right now** *or* **these days** *about each sentence.*

1. Prices are going up. _____these days_____

2. I'm coming. _____right now_____

3. I'm getting you some water. _____

4. We're getting in the car. _____

5. Camera phones are getting popular. _____

6. My girlfriend and I are fighting a lot. _____

7. The business is not making a lot of money. _____

8. I'm waking up early. _____

9. I'm studying. Please be quiet. _____

10. The students are not learning much. _____

4 | AFFIRMATIVE AND NEGATIVE STATEMENTS WITH THE PRESENT PROGRESSIVE

Write affirmative and negative sentences about each picture. Use the present progressive of the verb in parentheses.

1. (sleep) Marcus and Julius *are not sleeping*_____.

   (play) They *are playing*_____.

2. (stand) Mr. and Mrs. Bell _____ in the Ferris wheel.

   (sit) They _____ in the Ferris wheel.

3. (watch) Sue _____ TV.

   (read) Ted _____ a newspaper.

4. (read) Yukiko and Hiro _____ about Japan.

   (read) They _____ about Mexico.

5. (run) Luis _____.

   (stand) He _____.

6. (hold)   Berta _____ a camera phone.

   (talk)   She _____ on the phone.

7. (buy)   Yumi _____ food from a vending machine.

   (buy)   She _____ food at a supermarket.

8. (smile) Roberto and Marco _____.

   (cry)   They _____.

5 | AFFIRMATIVE AND NEGATIVE STATEMENTS WITH THE PRESENT PROGRESSIVE

Write true sentences.

1. I / do / a grammar exercise

   I am doing a grammar exercise. _____

2. I / sleep

   I am not sleeping. _____

3. I / have / a good time

   _____

4. The sun / shine

   _____

5. It / rain

   _____

(continued)

6. It / get / dark

_____

7. I / listen / to the radio

_____

8. I / talk / on the phone

_____

9. I / sit / on a chair

_____

10. My neighbors / make / a lot of noise

_____

6 | SUBJECT / VERB AGREEMENT WITH THE PRESENT PROGRESSIVE

Complete the postcard. Use the correct form of the verbs in parentheses.

January 11

    Greetings from Vermont from all of us. We are
_____ having _____ a great time. It
        1. (have)
_____ a little right now, and it
      2. (snow)
is cold. Many people _____ , but
         3. (ski)
we are too tired. We _____ at
         4. (relax)
the moment. Ellen and I _____ in
         5. (sit)
the coffee shop. She _____ , and
        6. (read)
I_____ to you! The girls
   7. (write)
_____ a snowman outside. They
     8. (make)
_____ themselves a lot. Naturally,
     9. (enjoy)
Tommy_____ a video game!
        10. (play)
    We hope you are well.

               Love from all of us,
               Nick

To:

Tom Gerardi
321 Maple Drive
Glen Oaks, NJ 02445

The Present Progressive: Yes/No and Wh- Questions

1 | YES/NO QUESTIONS WITH THE PRESENT PROGRESSIVE

Write questions. Then answer them. Use short answers. If you don't know an answer, write **I don't know**.

1. doing / you / a grammar exercise / Are

    Are you doing a grammar exercise?   Yes, I am.

2. glasses / wearing / you / Are

    _____   _____

3. your English teacher / correcting / Is / papers

    _____   _____

4. TV / you and a friend / watching /Are

    _____   _____

5. your classmates / doing / this exercise / now / Are

    _____   _____

6. Are / having / with your neighbors / dinner / you

    _____   _____

7. shining / the sun / Is

    _____   _____

8. your friends / Are / for you / waiting

    _____   _____

9. working / Are / your parents

    _____   _____

10. ice cream / eating / Are / you

    _____   _____

(continued)

11. Is / helping / your teacher / you

_____   _____

12. outside / children / Are / playing

_____   _____

2 | WH- QUESTIONS AND ANSWERS WITH PRESENT PROGRESSIVE

Look at the picture and answer the questions.

1. What is the little girl holding?   *A box of markers.*

2. Who is sleeping?   _____

3. Why is the man sleeping?   _____

4. Where is the little girl standing?   _____

5. What are the boys watching?   _____

6. Where are the boys sitting?   _____

7. Who is doing something wrong?   _____

3 | *YES / NO* QUESTIONS WITH THE PRESENT PROGRESSIVE

Write questions. Use the words in parentheses.

1. **A:** Yoko's in class.

   B: *Is she listening to the teacher?* _____ (listen to the teacher)

   A: Probably.

2. **A:** Mary's in the bedroom.

   B: _____ (sleep)

   A: Maybe.

3. **A:** All the children are at the playground.

   B: _____ (play)

   A: Probably.

4. **A:** My son and his friend are at the swimming pool.

   B: _____ (swim)

   A: I think so.

5. **A:** John's in the post office.

   B: _____ (buy stamps)

   A: Probably.

6. **A:** My parents are on vacation.

   B: _____ (have a good time)

   A: I hope so.

7. **A:** Carol's at the hospital.

   B: _____ (visit someone)

   A: I don't know.

8. **A:** Warren and Anne are outside.

   B: _____ (play tennis)

   A: I think so.

9. **A:** Julie's under the car.

   B: _____ (fix something)

   A: Maybe.

(continued)

10. **A:** Michael isn't here yet.

   B: _____ (come)

   A: I think so.

11. **A:** There are two people in the hall.

   B: _____ (wait for me)

   A: I don't know.

12. **A:** A man's behind you.

   B: _____ (follow me)

   A: I don't know.

4 | *WH-* QUESTIONS AND ANSWERS WITH THE PRESENT PROGRESSIVE

Write questions.

1. doing / you and Kevin / What / are

   What are you and Kevin doing?

2. watching / are / Why / you / a talk show

   _____

3. the people / are / talking about / What

   _____

4. Who / he / is / meeting

   _____

5. meeting / they / are / Where

   _____

6. are / Why / meeting / they / at the mall

   _____

7. laughing / is / Who

   _____

8. they / What / laughing about / are

   _____

9. sitting / you / Where / are

_____

10. are / you / What / eating

_____

5 | WH- QUESTIONS WITH THE PRESENT PROGRESSIVE

Write the correct questions from Exercise 4.

1. *Why are you watching a talk show?*

   Because it's interesting.

2. _____

   His old friends Peter Sanchez and Tommy Maguire.

3. _____

   I am watching a talk show. Kevin is meeting some people.

4. _____

   Ice cream.

5. _____

   Old movies.

6. _____

   Tommy works there.

7. _____

   Something funny in a movie.

8. _____

   In the living room.

9. _____

   The people on TV.

10. _____

   At the mall.

6 | *WHO* FOR SUBJECT OR OBJECT

Complete the conversations. Circle the correct answers and write them on the lines.

1. **A:** What are you doing?

   B: I'm talking on the phone.

   A: Who _____ *are you talking* _____ to?

        a. is talking   (**b.**) are you talking

   B: A friend.

2. **A:** What are you doing?

   B: I'm cooking for the party.

   A: Who _____ to the party?

        a. is coming   **b.** are they coming

   B: Some people from work.

3. **A:** Where's Conor?

   B: He's playing in the backyard.

   A: Who _____ with?

        a. is playing   **b.** is he playing

   B: Some friends from school.

4. **A:** The music is nice.

   B: Yes, it is.

   A: Who _____?

        a. is playing   **b.** is he playing

   B: My son.

5. **A:** What are you doing?

   B: I'm writing a letter.

   A: Who _____?

        a. is writing   **b.** are you writing to

   B: My cousin.

6. **A:** Are the kids at home?

   B: No, they're helping someone with some packages.

   A: Who _____?

       a. is helping   **b.** are they helping

   B: The older couple down the street.

7. **A:** Nurse Richards, is anybody still waiting in the office?

   B: Yes.

   A: Who _____?

       a. is waiting   **b.** are they waiting

   B: Ms. Gomez and Mr. Robertson.

7 | *WH-* QUESTIONS

Write questions.

1. **A:** Doug is painting something.

   B: *What is he painting?*

   A: I'm not sure. I think it's a portrait.

2. **A:** I'm reading.

   B: _____

   A: The newspaper.

3. **A:** The kids are eating.

   B: _____

   A: Some ice cream.

4. **A:** My husband's cooking.

   B: _____

   A: Dinner.

5. **A:** Someone's coming.

   B: _____

   A: I think it's your sister.

(continued)

6. **A:** I'm going to bed.

   B: _____

   A: I'm tired.

7. **A:** We're going.

   B: _____

   A: To the supermarket.

8. **A:** I'm selling my car.

   B: _____

   A: It's old.

9. **A:** Monica and Chris are swimming.

   B: _____

   A: In the pool near the park.

10. **A:** I'm watching TV.

    B: _____

    A: A baseball game.

11. **A:** The police officers are watching someone.

    B: _____

    A: That young man over there.

12. **A:** Jane's dating someone new.

    B: _____

    A: Eric Snyder.

The Imperative

1 | AFFIRMATIVE AND NEGATIVE IMPERATIVES

Match the people with their statements.

_d_ 1. The teacher said,   a. "Leave me alone."

____ 2. Mr. Michaels told his children,   b. "Open your mouth and say, 'Ah.'"

____ 3. The doctor said,   c. "Put your hands up."

____ 4. The police officer said,   d. "Open your books to page 34."

____ 5. Jenny told her brother,   e. "Go to bed."

Then do the same with these statements.

____ 6. The teacher said,   f. "Don't move."

____ 7. Mr. Michaels told his children,   g. "Don't eat so fast."

____ 8. The doctor said,   h. "Don't bother me."

____ 9. The police officer said,   i. "Don't talk during the test."

____ 10. Jenny told her brother,   j. "Don't take this medicine at night."

2 | AFFIRMATIVE AND NEGATIVE IMPERATIVES

*Complete the sentences. Use the verbs in the box. Add **Don't** where necessary.*

ask	be	buy	clean	give	~~go~~
~~open~~	study	talk	tell	touch	use

1. I'm hot. Please _____ _open_ _____ the window.

2. That animal is dangerous. _____ _Don't go_ _____ near it.

3. _____ your room right now. It's a mess.

4. The baby is asleep. _____ so loudly.

(continued)

5. The apples look bad. _____ them.

6. We're lost. _____ the police officer for directions.

7. It's a surprise party. _____ late.

8. This is a secret. _____ anyone.

9. The test is on Monday. _____ pages 50 and 51.

10. I'm cold. _____ me my sweater, please.

11. This glass isn't yours. _____ it.

12. The stove is hot. _____ it.

3 | AFFIRMATIVE IMPERATIVES

Look at the map and complete the note. Use the verbs in the box.

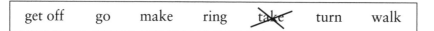

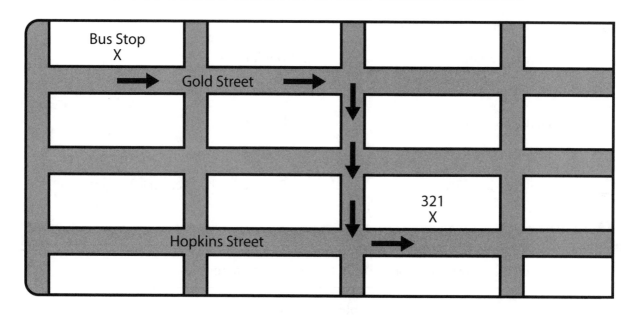

DIRECTIONS

_____*Take*_____ bus 26. _____ the bus on Gold Street.
      1.   **2.**

_____ down Gold Street. At the traffic light, _____ right.
    3.   **4.**

_____ another two blocks. Then _____ a left turn. That's Hopkins
    5.   **6.**

Street. _____ the bell at 321 Hopkins. That's my house.
       7.

4 | PHRASAL VERB IMPERATIVES

Replace the underlined word with the correct phrasal (two-word) verbs in parentheses.

          check out
1. Please ~~look at~~ our website for information about the trip.
(check in, check out, check up)

2. <u>Complete</u> the form with your name, address, and phone number.
(fill in, fill up)

3. You can <u>get</u> a form in the office near the door.
(pick on, pick out, pick up)

4. <u>Mail</u> the form before January 31st.
(send in, send on, send up)

1 | ABILITY

*Look at the job advertisements. Look at the qualifications of Martha, Frank, Les, and Rosa.
Then answer the questions.*

WANTED
SECRETARY
Good typing and computer skills.
Need to speak Spanish.

WANTED
SUMMER BABYSITTER
Take two small children to the beach everyday. Also, go horseback riding with 10-year-old girl.

DRIVER WANTED
Drive truck to airport every day.
Pick up boxes and deliver
to downtown offices.

WANTED
SUMMER CAMP WORKER
• Teach children the guitar
• Also work with children in art classes

	MARTHA	**FRANK**	**LES**	**ROSA**
draw	no	no	yes	yes
drive	yes	no	yes	no
lift 100 pounds	no	no	yes	yes
play the guitar	no	yes	no	yes
ride a horse	yes	no	no	no
speak Spanish	no	yes	no	yes
swim	yes	yes	no	yes
type	yes	yes	no	no

1. Which job is good for Martha? The job as a _____*summer babysitter*_____.

2. Which job is good for Frank? The job as a _____.

3. Which job is good for Les? The job as a _____.

4. Which job is good for Rosa? The job as a _____.

2 | AFFIRMATIVE AND NEGATIVE STATEMENTS WITH *CAN* FOR ABILITY

Look at the information in Exercise 1 again. Then answer the questions. Use **can** or **can't**.

1. Why is the job as babysitter good for Martha?

   She _can swim and ride a horse._ _____

2. Why isn't the job as babysitter good for Rosa?

   She _can swim, but she can't ride a horse._ _____

3. Why isn't the job as babysitter good for Les?

   He _can't swim, and he can't ride a horse._ _____

4. Why is the job as driver good for Les?

   He _____

5. Why is the job as secretary good for Frank?

   He _____

6. Why is the job as summer camp worker good for Rosa?

   She _____

7. Why isn't the job as driver good for Frank?

   He _____

8. Why isn't the job as secretary good for Martha?

   She _____

9. Why isn't the job as driver good for Rosa?

   She _____

10. Why isn't the job as summer camp worker good for Les?

    He _____

11. Why isn't the job as summer camp worker good for Martha?

    She _____

12. Why isn't the job as secretary good for Les?

    He _____

3 | *YES / NO* QUESTIONS WITH *CAN*

Write questions. Use **can**. *Then answer the questions. Use short answers.*

1. you / drive

   _Can you drive?_____   _Yes, I can. (OR No, I can't.)___

2. your mother / lift 100 pounds

   _____   _____

3. your father / play the guitar

   _____   _____

4. your best friend / ride a horse

   _____   _____

5. your parents / speak Spanish

   _____   _____

6. you / swim

   _____   _____

7. you / type

   _____   _____

4 | AFFIRMATIVE AND NEGATIVE STATEMENTS WITH *COULD* FOR PAST ABILITY

Complete the sentences. Use **could** *or* **couldn't** *and the verbs in parentheses.*

1. I'm sorry that I _____ _couldn't call_ _____ you yesterday. I was very busy.
                 (call)

2. We enjoyed our holiday in Spain because we _____ our Spanish.
                                              (practice)

3. We _____ to the party last night. Our son was sick.
             (go)

4. The test was really hard. I _____ all the questions.
                       (answer)

5. I had a bad stomachache yesterday. I _____ a thing.
                              (eat)

6. The work in high school was easy. I _____ soccer every weekend.
                                  (play)

7. The movie was sold out. We _____ any tickets.
                         (get)

8. Our hotel room wasn't good. We _____ the people in the other rooms.
                            (hear)

9. It wasn't warm on the weekend. We _____ swimming.
                          (go)

10. My summer vacation was great. I _____ whatever I wanted.
                            (do)

UNIT

19

Suggestions: *Let's, Why don't we . . . ?, Why don't you . . . ?; Responses*

1 | *LET'S* AND *WHY DON'T WE . . . ?*

Complete the sentences. Circle the correct answers and write them on the lines.

1. Students in an English class say to the teacher, " __Let's take a break.__ "

   a. Let's take a break.

   b. Let's take a test.

2. Donny says to his brother, "_____"

   a. Why don't we clean our room?

   b. Why don't we play basketball?

3. It's Saturday night, and Eric and Sylvia Chiu are tired. Sylvia says,

   "_____"

   a. Let's go dancing tonight.

   b. Let's not do anything tonight.

4. It's five o'clock. One secretary says to another secretary, "_____"

   a. Why don't we go out for dinner?

   b. Why don't we work late tonight?

5. Two tourists are in a foreign country. One tourist says to the other,

   "_____"

   a. Why don't we visit a museum?

   b. Why don't we sleep all day?

6. Louisa thinks TV is boring. She says to her boyfriend, "_____"

   a. Let's not watch TV tonight.

   b. Let's watch TV tonight.

(continued)

7. It's a beautiful day. Miriam says to her roommate, "_____"

    a. Let's not forget our umbrellas.

    b. Let's not take the car to class today. Let's walk.

8. It's Frederico's birthday. His wife says to their daughter, "_____"

    a. Why don't we get a present for Dad?

    b. Why don't we forget about Dad's birthday?

9. Celia and her sister are late. Celia says, "_____"

    a. Let's take a taxi.

    b. Let's walk.

10. It's cold. Jenny says to her boyfriend, "_____"

    a. Let's wait outside.

    b. Let's not wait outside.

2 | LET'S AND *WHY DON'T WE* . . . ?

Write sentences. Use **let's** *and the expressions in the box.*

get something to eat	go swimming	leave
go inside	~~go to bed~~	not invite her to the party
go out and look for him		

1. **A:** I'm tired.

    B: I am, too.

    A: *Let's go to bed.* _____

2. **A:** I'm hungry.

    B: I am, too.

    A: _____

3. **A:** I'm hot.

    B: I am, too.

    A: _____

4. A: I'm angry with Mariana.

   B: I am, too.

   A: _____

Write sentences. Use **Why don't we . . . ?** *and the expressions in the box.*

5. A: I'm worried about Rocky. Where is he?

   B: I don't know.

   A: _____

6. A: I'm cold.

   B: I am, too.

   A: _____

7. A: I'm bored at this party.

   B: I am, too.

   A: _____

3 | WHY DON'T YOU . . . ?

Match the sentences and responses.

__c__ 1. I'm tired.

_____ 2. I don't know the meaning of this word.

_____ 3. I don't know what to do tonight.

_____ 4. I'm hungry.

_____ 5. I'm hot.

a. Why don't you make a sandwich?

b. Why don't you go to the movies?

c. Why don't you go to bed?

d. Why don't you open the window?

e. Why don't you look it up in your dictionary?

Write your own responses with **Why don't you . . . ?**

6. I'm bored.

_____

7. I want to practice English more.

_____

8. I have a headache.

_____

4 | SUGGESTIONS AND RESPONSES WITH *WHY DON'T WE* AND *LET'S* . . .

Complete the conversations. Use the words in the box.

can't	don't	~~idea~~	instead
it	OK	plan	Sorry
Sounds	~~That's~~	Why	

1. **A:** Let's go to the movies.

   B: _____*That's*_____ a good _____*idea*_____.

2. **A:** Why don't we go out for dinner?

   B: No, I _____ feel like _____.

3. **A:** Let's go to a Chinese restaurant for lunch.

   B: _____ don't we go to a Mexican restaurant _____?

4. **A:** Let's go to New York for a few days.

   B: _____, I _____. I'm really busy at work.

5. **A:** Let's stay at home tonight.

   B: _____.

6. **A:** Why don't we visit your sister and her family next weekend?

   B: Sounds like a _____.

7. **A:** Let's not take a taxi.

   B: _____ good to me. I like to walk.

UNIT

20

The Simple Past: Regular Verbs—Affirmative and Negative Statements

1 | SIMPLE PAST: REGULAR VERBS—AFFIRMATIVE AND NEGATIVE STATEMENTS

Match the sentences.

_d_ **1.** Sylvia is tired.

_____ **2.** Sylvia's worried about her French test.

_____ **3.** Sylvia's car is clean.

_____ **4.** Sylvia is hungry.

_____ **5.** Sylvia is angry.

_____ **6.** Sylvia is happy.

_____ **7.** Sylvia's talking about a TV program.

_____ **8.** Sylvia's grandparents are unhappy.

_____ **9.** There's a lot of food in Sylvia's refrigerator.

a. She washed it yesterday.

b. Her boyfriend called her yesterday to say, "I love you."

c. She watched it last night.

d. She didn't sleep much last night.

e. She didn't eat breakfast or lunch.

f. She didn't visit them last weekend.

g. Her boyfriend forgot her birthday.

h. She cooked a lot yesterday.

i. She didn't study very much.

2 | PAST TIME MARKERS

Complete the sentences. Use **yesterday** *or* **last**.

Detective's Notes on Mr. Horace Smith

April 15th Traveled to Vancouver

April 25th Borrowed #20,000

May 13th Moved into new apartment

(Nothing unusual until May 19th)

May 19th
7:00 A.M.   Arrived at work
2:00 P.M.   Finished work
6:00 P.M.   Returned to the office
11:00 P.M.   Visited someone at a hotel

It's Thursday, May 20th. Here's our report on Horace Smith.

_____Last_____ month he traveled to Vancouver. _____
    1.   **2.**
month he also borrowed $20,000 from the bank. _____ week he moved
                                                          3.
into a new apartment. _____ morning he arrived at work at seven
                                4.
o'clock. At two o'clock _____ afternoon he finished work. Then
                                5.
something strange happened. He returned to the office at six o'clock _____
                                                                              6.
evening and visited someone at a hotel at eleven o'clock _____ night.
                                                                    7.

3 | SIMPLE PAST AND *AGO*

Answer the questions.

a. What day of the week is it today? _____

b. What month is it now?   _____

c. What year is it now?   _____

*Use the answers at the bottom of page 80 to rewrite the sentences. Use **ago**.*

1. Karen washed her car last Saturday. (*Answer as though today is Monday.*)

   Karen washed her car two days ago.

2. Karen learned how to drive in 2000.

   _____

3. Karen visited her high school friends last May.

   _____

4. Karen called her grandparents last Monday.

   _____

5. Karen talked to her parents last Friday.

   _____

6. Karen shared an apartment with friends in 2001.

   _____

7. Karen traveled to Hong Kong last December.

   _____

8. Karen invited some friends for dinner last Wednesday.

   _____

9. Karen worked in Miami in 2002.

   _____

10. Karen started her own business last September.

    _____

4 | AFFIRMATIVE STATEMENTS WITH THE SIMPLE PAST

Complete the sentences. Use subject pronouns.

1. Pete walks to work every day.

   _____ *He walked to work* _____ yesterday, too.

2. Lenny, Mike, and Warren play basketball every Saturday.

   _____ last Saturday, too.

(continued)

3. Ellen washes her clothes every Sunday.

   _____ last Sunday, too.

4. My classmates study every night.

   _____ last night, too.

5. Robert works in his garden every weekend.

   _____ last weekend, too.

6. Norman cooks dinner at 6:00 every day.

   _____ yesterday, too.

7. Anna talks to her daughter every Friday night.

   _____ last Friday night, too.

8. Michele and her husband travel to France every summer.

   _____ last summer, too.

9. The bank closes at 3:00 P.M. every day.

   _____ yesterday, too.

10. Adam and his sister watch TV every night.

    _____ last night, too.

5 | AFFIRMATIVE AND NEGATIVE STATEMENTS WITH THE SIMPLE PAST

Complete the sentences. Use the correct form of the verbs in parentheses.

1. I _____*watched*_____ TV last night, but I _____*didn't watch*_____ a movie.
        (watch)   (not watch)

2. We _____ our lunch at the hotel yesterday, but we _____
        (enjoy)   (not enjoy)
   our dinner.

3. I _____ you on Monday, but I _____ you on Tuesday.
       (e-mail)   (not e-mail)

4. James _____ late on Thursday, but he _____ late on Friday.
          (arrive)   (not arrive)

5. Monica _____ to call last Saturday, but she _____ to come.
           (promise)   (not promise)

6. We _____ Toronto last year, but we _____ Montreal.
       (visit)   (not visit)

7. Lucy _____ to change her ticket, but she _____ to change
         (try)   (not try)
   her husband's ticket.

8. We _____ a lot yesterday morning, but we _____ a lot
   (walk)   (not walk)

   yesterday afternoon.

9. Jerry _____ Alice at the party, but he _____ Barbara.
   (hug)   (not hug)

10. They _____ a car last week, but they _____ a big car.
    (rent)   (not rent)

6 | VERB REVIEW: PRESENT PROGRESSIVE, SIMPLE PRESENT, AND SIMPLE PAST

Complete the letter. Use the simple present, present progressive, or simple past of the verbs in parentheses.

> *April 12*
>
> Dear Amira,
>
> I _____am sitting_____ at my desk, and I _____ of you. I often
>   1. (sit)   2. (think)
>
> _____ of you on days like today. The sun _____ , and the
>   3. (think)   4. (shine)
>
> birds _____ .
>   5. (sing)
>
> The weather's very different from the weather yesterday. It _____
>   6. (rain)
>
> all day long, and I _____ in the house from morning until night. I
>   7. (stay)
>
> _____ out at all. I _____ the clothes and _____
>   8. (not go)   9. (wash)   10. (clean)
>
> the house—very exciting! After dinner, I _____ cards with some neighbors.
>   11. (play)
>
> One of my neighbors, Alfredo, _____ from Argentina. Sometimes I
>   12. (come)
>
> _____ Spanish with him. I _____ Spanish very well, but
>   13. (speak)   14. (not speak)
>
> Alfredo is very nice and never _____ at my mistakes.
>   15. (laugh)
>
> Last week he _____ me to an Argentinian party. We
>   16. (invite)
>
> _____ to beautiful music all night, and I _____ a lot. I really
>   17. (listen)   18. (dance)
>
> _____ myself.
>   19. (enjoy)
>
> Well, it's time to go. I _____ some Argentinian food, and I
>   20. (cook)
>
> _____ to check it. I _____ it to burn. You and I both
>   21. (need)   22. (not want)
>
> _____ that I'm not a very good cook!
>   23. (know)
>
> Write soon!
>
>   Love,
>   Connie

21 The Simple Past: Irregular Verbs—Affirmative and Negative Statements

1 | REGULAR AND IRREGULAR VERBS

Underline the simple past verb form in each sentence. Write **regular** *if it is regular. Write* **irregular** *if it is irregular. Then write the base form of the verb.*

1. This morning I <u>got</u> up at seven o'clock.   <u>irregular</u>   <u>get</u>

2. I <u>washed</u> my face and hands.   <u>regular</u>   <u>wash</u>

3. Then I put on my clothes. _____ _____

4. I had orange juice and toast for breakfast. _____ _____

5. After breakfast I brushed my teeth. _____ _____

6. I left the house at 7:45. _____ _____

7. I arrived at school at 8:15. _____ _____

8. Class began at 8:30. _____ _____

9. We learned some new grammar rules in class today. _____ _____

10. Class finished at 11:30. _____ _____

11. I met some friends for lunch. _____ _____

12. We ate at a pizza place. _____ _____

13. After lunch we went to a swimming pool. _____ _____

14. We stayed there until four o'clock. _____ _____

2 | AFFIRMATIVE STATEMENTS WITH THE SIMPLE PAST OF IRREGULAR VERBS

Complete each sentence with the simple past form of the verb.

1. I didn't see Miguel. I _____*saw*_____ Carlos.

2. I didn't get up at 6:00. I _____ up at 7:00.

3. We didn't eat dinner at home. We _____ dinner at a restaurant.

4. She didn't put the bag in the bedroom. She _____ it in the kitchen.

5. Ming didn't go shopping on Saturday. He _____ shopping on Friday.

6. I didn't have eggs for breakfast. I _____ a sandwich.

7. Dr. Wu didn't say that. Dr. Gomez _____ it.

8. Louisa didn't know all the answers. She only _____ three.

9. We didn't meet any people from Mexico, but we _____ people from Peru.

10. Jack London didn't come to the party. His wife _____ instead.

11. Adam and Paula didn't sell their TV. They _____ their computer.

12. Mr. Daly didn't teach math. He _____ history.

13. Nick and Jenna didn't leave yesterday. They _____ three days ago.

14. I didn't buy a shirt. I _____ a hat.

15. The movie didn't begin at 8:00. It _____ at 7:45.

3 | NEGATIVE STATEMENTS WITH THE SIMPLE PAST OF IRREGULAR VERBS

Write true sentences.

1. I / become / an English teacher / last year

   I didn't become an English teacher last year.

2. I / eat / 3 kilos of oranges for breakfast / yesterday morning

   _____

3. I / sleep / 21 hours / yesterday

   _____

4. I / bring / a horse to English class / two weeks ago

   _____

5. I / go / to the moon / last month

   _____

6. I / meet / the leader of my country / last night

   _____

7. I / find / $10,000 in a brown paper bag / yesterday

   _____

8. I / do / this exercise / two years ago

   _____

9. I / swim / 30 kilometers / yesterday

   _____

10. I / speak / English perfectly / 10 years ago

   _____

4 | AFFIRMATIVE AND NEGATIVE STATEMENTS WITH THE SIMPLE PAST

Complete the diary. Use the simple past form of the verbs in parentheses.

I _____had_____ a nice day today. I _____ up until ten
    1. (have)   **2. (not get)**
o'clock, so I _____ dressed quickly and _____ to the
    3. (get)   **4. (go)**
Fine Arts Museum.

    I _____ Cindy and Frank there, and we _____
    5. (meet)   **6. (go)**
into the museum to see a new exhibit. We _____ everything because
    7. (not see)
we _____ enough time. The exhibit _____ at one o'clock.
    8. (not have)   **9. (close)**
    We _____ at a Chinese restaurant near the museum, and then
    10. (eat)
we _____ a bus to the Downtown Shopping Mall. We
    11. (take)
_____ at the mall for a couple of hours and _____
    12. (stay)   **13. (look)**
around. I _____ a new shirt, but Frank and Cindy
    14. (buy)
_____ anything.
    15. (not buy)
    Cindy and Frank _____ back home with me, and I
    16. (come)
_____ dinner here. I _____ much in the refrigerator,
    17. (make)   **18. (not have)**
so I _____ to the supermarket to get some things. I
    19. (drive)
_____ Ramón there and _____ him for dinner, too.
    20. (see)   **21. (invite)**
    We _____ until late, and after dinner we _____
    22. (not eat)   **23. (watch)**
a video. Ramón, Cindy, and Frank _____ until after midnight.
    24. (not leave)
    It's one o'clock in the morning now, and I'm tired. It's time to go to bed.

Good night!

1 | YES/NO QUESTIONS AND SHORT ANSWERS WITH THE SIMPLE PAST

Read the information about William Shakespeare. Answer the questions. Use short answers.

William Shakespeare, 1564–1616	Place of birth and death: Stratford-upon-Avon, England
Married Anne Hathaway, 1582	Daughter Susanna, born in 1583
Moved to London without family after 1585; worked there as actor and playwright until 1610	Twins Hamnet and Judith, born in 1585
	Wrote over 35 plays and 154 poems

1. Did Shakespeare work in London?   *Yes, he did.* _____

2. Did Shakespeare live in London? _____

3. Did Shakespeare have any children? _____

4. Did Shakespeare's family live with him in London? _____

5. Did Shakespeare write a lot of plays? _____

6. Did Shakespeare work as an actor? _____

7. Did Shakespeare's wife have five children? _____

8. Did Shakespeare die in London? _____

2 | EDITING

Correct the mistake in each question. Write the correct questions. Use short answers.

1. You did finish the last exercise?

   Did you finish the last exercise?

   Yes, I did. (OR *No, I didn't.*)

2. Did you all the homework?

   _____

   _____

3. You did took a bath this morning?

   _____

   _____

4. Does your best friend come over to your house last night?

   _____

   _____

5. Did you went to bed early last night?

   _____

   _____

6. Did your English teacher taught you new grammar last week?

   _____

   _____

7. Do you visit the United States 10 years ago?

   _____

   _____

8. Did your mother and father got married a long time ago?

   _____

   _____

9. Did you watched TV last night?

   _____

   _____

3 | AFFIRMATIVE STATEMENTS AND *YES/NO* QUESTIONS WITH THE SIMPLE PAST

Look at Sharon's list. Write her husband's questions. Then complete each answer. Use the simple past form of the verbs in parentheses.

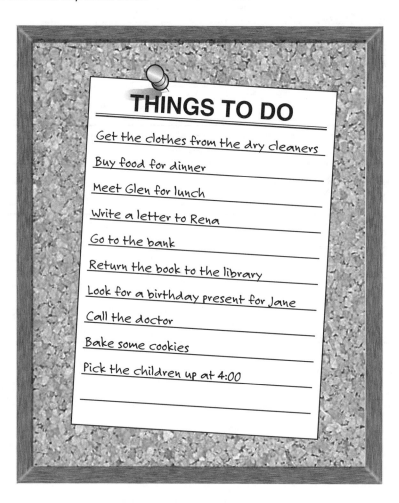

THINGS TO DO

Get the clothes from the dry cleaners

Buy food for dinner

Meet Glen for lunch

Write a letter to Rena

Go to the bank

Return the book to the library

Look for a birthday present for Jane

Call the doctor

Bake some cookies

Pick the children up at 4:00

SHARON: Steven, you always say I forget to do things. Well, today I remembered to do everything.

STEVEN: Are you sure? Let's see your list. ___*Did you get the clothes from the dry cleaners?*___
                                                                                        1.

SHARON: Uh-huh. I _____*put*_____ them in the closet.
                              2. (put)

STEVEN: _____
                                        3.

SHARON: Yes, I did. I _____ some chicken, some vegetables, and some apples
                                   4. (get)

for dessert.

STEVEN: _____
                                        5.

SHARON: Yeah. We _____ at a great Thai restaurant.
                              6. (eat)

STEVEN: _____
                                        7.

SHARON: Yes. I _____ it at the post office.
                    8. (mail)

STEVEN: _____
                                    9.

SHARON: Yes, I did. I _____ both of the checks.
                          10. (deposit)

STEVEN: _____
                                    11.

SHARON: Yes, I did. And I _____ out another book by the same author.
                              12. (take)

STEVEN: _____
                                    13.

SHARON: Yeah. I _____ her a sweater.
                    14. (buy)

STEVEN: _____
                                    15.

SHARON: Uh-huh. He _____ all the test results are fine.
                        16. (say)

STEVEN: _____
                                    17.

SHARON: Of course. And I _____ a few already. They're delicious.
                              18. (have)

STEVEN: _____
                                    19.

SHARON: Oh no, I _____! What time is it?
                      20. (forget)

4 | WH- QUESTIONS WITH THE SIMPLE PAST

Match the questions and answers.

_e_ 1. Who wrote *The Merchant of Venice*?

____ 2. When did the movie *The Merchant of Venice* come out?

____ 3. Who did you see the movie with?

____ 4. Why did you go to see the movie?

____ 5. How long did it take you to read the play?

____ 6. Who starred in the movie?

____ 7. Where did you see the movie?

____ 8. What did you think of the movie?

____ 9. When did Shakespeare write *The Merchant of Venice*?

a. Al Pacino and Jeremy Irons.

b. My roommate.

c. Hundreds of years ago.

d. At home on a DVD.

e. Shakespeare.

f. In 2005.

g. Because I like the play.

h. It was pretty good.

i. About a month.

5 | *WH-* QUESTIONS WITH THE SIMPLE PAST

Write questions. Then answer them. (If you need help, the answers are at the end of the exercise, but they are not in order.)

1. Where / Arnold Schwarzenegger / grow up

   Where did Arnold Schwarzenegger grow up?

   In Austria.

2. When / a person / walk on the moon / for the first time

   _____

   _____

3. What / William Shakespeare / write

   _____

   _____

4. Where / the Olympic games / start

   _____

   _____

5. Why / many people / go to California / in 1849

   _____

   _____

6. How long / Bill Clinton / live in the White House

   _____

   _____

7. What / Alfred Hitchcock / make

   _____

   _____

8. Why / the Chinese / build the Great Wall

   _____

   _____

9. How long / World War II / last in Europe

_____

_____

10. When / Christopher Columbus / sail to / America

_____

_____

About six years.

Eight years.

In 1492.

In 1969.

~~In Austria.~~

In Greece.

Movies.

Plays like *Romeo and Juliet*.

They wanted to find gold.

They wanted to keep foreigners out of the country.

6 | QUESTIONS WITH *WHO* AS SUBJECT OR OBJECT

Write questions. Use **who** *and the verb in parentheses.*

1. A: I went to San Francisco during my vacation.

    B: _____*Who did you go*_____ with?
                    (go)

    A: My friends Adam and Jean.

    B: How did you get there?

    A: By car.

    B: _____*Who drove*_____?
               (drive)

    A: We all did.

2. A: Those are beautiful flowers. _____ them to you?
                                   (give)

    B: My boyfriend.

(continued)

3. **A:** I went to a party at my old high school last night.

   B: _____ there?
   <u>(see)</u>

   A: I saw a few old friends.

4. **A:** You got a phone call a couple of minutes ago.

   B: _____?
   <u>(call)</u>

   A: A woman. Her name was Betty Kowalski.

5. **A:** Did you ever read the book *The Old Man and the Sea*?

   B: _____ it?
   <u>(write)</u>

   A: Ernest Hemingway.

6. **A:** Where are the children?

   B: At Ryan Santiago's house.

   A: _____ them there?
   <u>(take)</u>

   B: Ryan's mother.

7. **A:** My wife sent the money to your office a month ago.

   B: _____ it to?
   <u>(send)</u>

   A: Nicole Sanda.

8. **A:** The car is so clean. _____ it?
   <u>(clean)</u>

   B: I took it to a car wash.

   A: It looks great.

9. **A:** Did you hear the news? Kay got married.

   B: Really? _____?
   <u>(marry)</u>

   A: A guy from Oklahoma. I don't know his name.

10. **A:** My grandparents went to Arizona for two months last winter.

    B: _____ with?
    <u>(stay)</u>

    A: My cousin, Howard. He has a big house there.

There Is / There Are;
Is There . . .? /
Are There . . .?

---

1 | **AFFIRMATIVE STATEMENTS WITH *THERE IS* AND *THERE ARE***

Complete the conversation. Use **there is** *or* **there are**.

A: Is anyone in the house?

B: Yes, _____there are_____ two men. _____ also a woman. Oh,
                  1.   **2.**
_____ two little boys, too.
        3.

A: And in the yard?

B: _____ a dog, and _____ three other children.
              4.   **5.**

A: What's in the garage?

B: _____ some boxes.
              6.

A: What's in them?

B: I don't know, but _____ also a motorcycle. _____ two cars, too.
                                7.   **8.**

A: Two?

B: Uh-huh. _____ a TV there, too.
                      9.

A: A TV? In the garage? That's strange.

B: And _____ a sofa.
                10.

A: That's really strange!

2 | AFFIRMATIVE STATEMENTS WITH *THERE IS* AND *THERE ARE*

Write sentences.

1. stores / the mall / are / in / There

   There are stores in the mall.

2. is / computer / a / There / in / the store

   _____

3. the first floor / There / restaurants / on / are / two

   _____

4. people / There / the door / at / are

   _____

5. sweater / the bag / is / in / a / There

   _____

6. between / There / the cafés / a / is / bookstore

   _____

7. are / There / the menu / on / burgers

   _____

8. are / There / the floor / boxes / on

   _____

9. five / near / There / the man and woman / children / are

   _____

3 | AFFIRMATIVE STATEMENTS WITH *THERE IS* AND *THERE ARE*

What's for sale at the yard sale? Write sentences. Use **there is** *or* **there are**.

1. *There is a telephone for sale.*
2. *There are suitcases for sale.*
3. _____
4. _____
5. _____
6. _____
7. _____
8. _____
9. _____
10. _____
11. _____
12. _____
13. _____

4 AFFIRMATIVE STATEMENTS WITH *THERE IS, THERE ISN'T, THERE ARE,* AND *THERE AREN'T*

Write sentences about Vacation Hotel. Use **there is**, **there isn't**, **there are**, *or* **there aren't**.

VACATION HOTEL

In every room:
○ *a bathroom*
○ *two beds*
○ *two closets*
○ *a TV*
○ *an air conditioner*

At the hotel:
○ *two restaurants*
○ *four tennis courts*
○ *two parking lots*

1. (a bathroom in every room)   *There is a bathroom in every room.*

2. (a radio in every room)   *There isn't a radio in every room.*

3. (two beds in every room)   _____

4. (two closets in every room)   _____

5. (a telephone in every room)   _____

6. (a television in every room)   _____

7. (an air conditioner in every room) _____

8. (a refrigerator in every room)   _____

9. (a swimming pool at the hotel)   _____

10. (two restaurants at the hotel)   _____

11. (four tennis courts at the hotel) _____

12. (gift shops at the hotel)   _____

13. (two parking lots at the hotel) _____

5 AFFIRMATIVE STATEMENTS WITH *THERE ARE, THERE AREN'T, THEY ARE,* AND *THEY AREN'T*

Write sentences. Use **there are**, **there aren't**, **they are**, *or* **they aren't** *and the information below.*

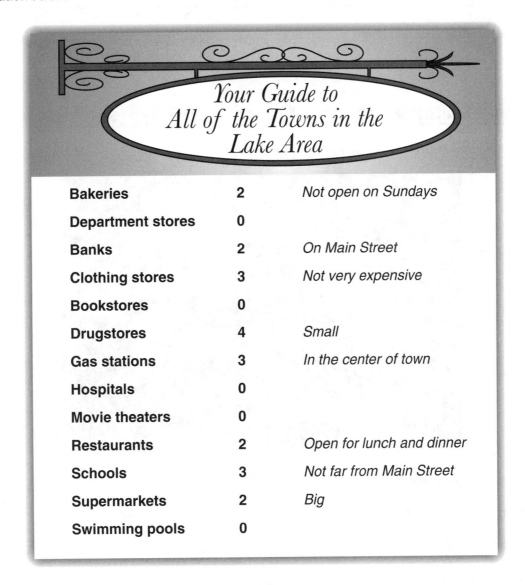

Your Guide to
All of the Towns in the
Lake Area

Bakeries	2	Not open on Sundays
Department stores	0	
Banks	2	On Main Street
Clothing stores	3	Not very expensive
Bookstores	0	
Drugstores	4	Small
Gas stations	3	In the center of town
Hospitals	0	
Movie theaters	0	
Restaurants	2	Open for lunch and dinner
Schools	3	Not far from Main Street
Supermarkets	2	Big
Swimming pools	0	

1. *There are two bakeries. They aren't open on Sundays.* _____

2. *There aren't any department stores.* _____

3. _____

4. _____

5. _____

6. _____

7. _____

(continued)

8. _____

9. _____

10. _____

11. _____

12. _____

13. _____

6 | YES/NO QUESTIONS WITH *ARE THERE* AND SHORT ANSWERS

Look at the picture. Answer the questions. Use short answers.

1. Are there any stores? _Yes, there are._

2. Are there any people? _____

3. Are there any dogs? _____

4. Are there any children? _____

5. Are there any flowers? _____

6. Are there any restaurants? _____

7. Are there any trees? _____

8. Are there any police officers? _____

9. Are there any stairs? _____

7 | YES/NO QUESTIONS WITH *IS THERE* AND *ARE THERE* AND SHORT ANSWERS

Write questions. Then answer them.

1. many elephants in Florida

   Are there many elephants in Florida?   No, there aren't.

2. many elephants in India

   _____   _____

3. a desert in Canada

   _____   _____

4. camels in Saudi Arabia

   _____   _____

5. a long river in the Sahara Desert

   _____   _____

6. many lions in Russia

   _____   _____

7. mountains in Kenya

   _____   _____

8. many people in Antarctica

   _____   _____

9. big city in Thailand

   _____   _____

10. a monkey in your garden

   _____   _____

8 | *THERE, IT, SHE, AND THEY*

Complete the conversation. Use **there, there's, it's, she's, they're,** *or* **there are**.

A: Is _____there_____ an office supply store in this mall?
     _{1.}

B: Yes, _____ is. _____ next to the bookstore.
     _{2.}   _{3.}
Why? What do you want to get?

A: _____ a problem with my computer, so I'm thinking about getting a
     _{4.}
new one.

B: Oh, _____ aren't any computers in the office supply store. But
     _{5.}
_____ an electronics store in the mall. _____
     _{6.}   _{7.}
on the second floor.

A: Do you mind if we go there?

B: No, let's go. _____ some stairs near here.
     _{8.}
_____ near the Food Court.
     _{9.}

[A few minutes later in the electronics store.]

A: So where are the computers?

B: I think _____ in the back of the store, but I'm not sure.
     _{10.}

A: _____ a saleswoman. Let's ask her.
     _{11.}

B: Where?

A: Over there. _____ wearing a yellow T-shirt.
     _{12.}

Subject and Object Pronouns; Direct and Indirect Objects

1 | DIRECT OBJECTS

Underline the object in each sentence.

1. Please help <u>Mr. and Mrs. Liu</u>.

2. Let's buy some chocolate.

3. Write two paragraphs.

4. Don't read your e-mail.

5. Don't drink the coffee.

6. Open the door.

2 | OBJECT PRONOUNS

Underline the object pronoun in each sentence.

1. I called <u>them</u>.

2. I like you a lot.

3. My sister likes him a lot.

4. Send it tomorrow.

5. E-mail her now.

6. His brother bought them.

7. Why don't you show us?

8. She wrote me.

3 | SUBJECT PRONOUNS, POSSESSIVE ADJECTIVES, AND OBJECT PRONOUNS

Complete the chart.

	SUBJECT PRONOUNS (*I* am here.)	POSSESSIVE ADJECTIVES (This is *my* book.)	OBJECT PRONOUNS (Help *me*.)
1.	I	my	
2.		your	you
3.	he		him
4.		her	
5.	it		
6.		our	
7.	they		

4 | OBJECT PRONOUNS

Complete the sentences. Use **me, you, him, her, us,** *or* **them.**

1. **A:** Is this for Mr. Berger?

   B: Yes, it's for _____ *him* _____.

2. **A:** Is this for you and your wife?

   B: Yes, it's for _____.

3. **A:** Is this for your brother and sister?

   B: Yes, it's for _____.

4. **A:** Is this for me?

   B: Yes, it's for _____.

5. **A:** Is this for Maria?

   B: Yes, it's for _____.

6. **A:** Is this for Chris and me?

   B: Yes, it's for _____.

7. **A:** Is this for Ms. McGowan?

   B: Yes, it's for _____.

8. **A:** Is this for my neighbors?

   B: Yes, it's for _____.

9. **A:** Is this for you and Ari?

   B: Yes, it's for _____.

10. **A:** Is this for Anna's boyfriend?

    B: Yes, it's for _____.

11. **A:** Is this for the horses?

    B: Yes, it's for _____.

12. **A:** Is this for John?

    B: Yes, it's for _____.

5 | SUBJECT AND OBJECT PRONOUNS

Unscramble the word groups to write sentences. Use correct punctuation and capitalization.

1. love / you / I   *I love you.*_____

2. him / She / loves   _____

3. us / love / They   _____

4. We / them / love   _____

5. the answer / Tell / me _____

6. Show / her / the paper _____

7. them / Take / some flowers _____

8. me / a postcard / Send   _____

6 | SUBJECT AND OBJECT PRONOUNS

Complete the sentences. Use a subject pronoun or an object pronoun.

1. **A:** Is your name Doug?

   B: Yes, _____ *it* _____ is.

2. **A:** This CD is for you. _____'s for your birthday.

   B: Oh, thank you. I love _____.

3. **A:** Is Maryann your aunt?

   B: Yes, _____ is.

   A: Please give _____ this package.

4. **A:** My brother is over there.

   B: I like _____. _____ is handsome.

5. **A:** Are you busy?

   B: Yes, _____ am. Please call _____ later.

6. **A:** Here are two dishes.

   B: But _____'re dirty. Please wash _____.

(continued)

7. **A:** Are you and Lee free on Sunday?

B: Yes, _____ are. Visit _____ then.

8. **A:** Hello?

B: Hello. Is Judi there?

A: Yes. Just a minute. Judi! Judi! The phone's for _____.

7 | DIRECT AND INDIRECT OBJECT WORD ORDER

Who probably said each of the sentences? Match the sentences and speakers.

__f__ 1. "Please show me your driver's license."

_____ 2. "I explained the answers to you in the last class."

_____ 3. "Please send this letter to Korea."

_____ 4. "Let's e-mail this joke to Bill. It's funny."

_____ 5. "Please pass me the salt and pepper."

_____ 6. "Read the story to me again, please."

_____ 7. "Give me your passport, please."

_____ 8. "I sent the information to you two days ago."

a. an immigration officer

b. a child

c. a restaurant customer

d. someone at an office

e. a teacher

f. a police officer

g. a post office customer

h. a friend

8 | DIRECT AND INDIRECT OBJECT WORD ORDER

Write the direct object and indirect object in each sentence in Exercise 7.

Direct Object	Indirect Object
1. *your driver's license*	*me*
2.	
3.	
4.	
5.	
6.	
7.	
8.	

9 | DIRECT AND INDIRECT OBJECT WORD ORDER

Bernie came home for a visit a few days ago. He gave the following gifts to his family and friends.

Gifts

Lucy—a sweater

Bob—a CD

his brother—a video game

Marge—some earrings

his grandfather—some pajamas

Bill   a book

his cousin—some sunglasses

his girlfriend—a ring

Write sentences about Bernie. Use the information in the box. Put the indirect object before the direct object.

1. *Bernie gave Lucy a sweater.*

2. *He gave*

3. _____

4. _____

Write more sentences about Bernie. Use the information in the box. Put the direct object before the indirect object.

5. *He gave some pajamas to his grandfather.*

6. _____

7. _____

8. _____

10 | DIRECT AND INDIRECT OBJECT PRONOUNS

Complete the sentences. Use the correct preposition and **it**, **them**, **me**, **him**, *or* **her**.

1. This is Robert's cell phone. Give __*it to him*_____.

2. This is Tony and Nicole's gift. Send _____.

3. These are my sister's CDs. Give _____.

4. Those are your father's keys. Hand _____.

5. Julia needs the eraser. Pass _____.

6. I want to see the pictures. Show _____.

11 | DIRECT AND INDIRECT OBJECT WORD ORDER

Write sentences. Use correct punctuation and capitalization.

1. lent / him / some money / I

    *I lent him some money.*_____

2. to / some money / I / him / lent

    _____

3. the women / The man / something / is / to / showing

    _____

4. them / She / some help / gives / always

    _____

5. you / tell / the answer / him / Did / ?

    _____

6. all my friends / birthday cards / I / send

    _____

7. to / the ball / me / Throw

    _____

8. this sentence / us / didn't / You / to / explain

    _____

9. me / He / fifty dollars / owes

    _____

Count and Non-Count Nouns; Articles

1 | COUNT NOUNS AND NON-COUNT NOUNS

Look at the store signs. Write the correct aisle number.

1	Eggs / Juice / Milk / Butter / Cheese
2	Bread / Rolls
3	Toothbrushes / Toothpaste / Soap / Shampoo
4	Toilet Paper / Paper Towels / Napkins / Plastic Bags
5	Potato Chips / Cookies / Cereal

6	Sugar / Flour / Salt
7	Frozen Food / Ice Cream
8	Canned Vegetables / Canned Fish / Rice
9	Fresh Fruit

1. <u>Sugar</u> is in aisle __6__.

2. <u>Cookies</u> are in aisle ____.

3. <u>Ice cream</u> is in aisle ____.

4. <u>Eggs</u> are in aisle ____.

5. <u>Fruit</u> is in aisle ____.

6. Canned <u>vegetables</u> are in aisle ____.

7. <u>Napkins</u> are in aisle ____.

8. <u>Milk</u> is in aisle ____.

9. <u>Rice</u> is in aisle ____.

10. Plastic <u>bags</u> are in aisle ____.

11. <u>Potato chips</u> are in aisle ____.

12. Frozen <u>food</u> is in aisle ____.

13. <u>Bread</u> is in aisle ____.

14. Canned <u>fish</u> is in aisle ____.

15. <u>Toothbrushes</u> are in aisle ____.

2 | COUNT NOUNS AND NON-COUNT NOUNS

Write the underlined words in Exercise 1 in the correct column.

Count Nouns	Non-count Nouns
cookies	sugar

3 | COUNT NOUNS AND NON-COUNT NOUNS

*Circle the twelve words that don't belong in the lists of count nouns and non-count nouns. Then write correct lists. Write **a**, **an**, or **some** before each word.*

Count Nouns	Non-count Nouns	Count Nouns	Non-count Nouns
egg	books	an egg	some bread
bread	food	some books	some food
furniture	water		
student	people		
money	paper		
information	uncle		
teeth	homework		
rain	advice		
children	cell phone		
friends	traffic		
oil	questions		
animal	computer		

4 | COUNT NOUNS AND NON-COUNT NOUNS

Complete the sentences. Circle the correct answers and write them on the lines.

1. Does the baby want _____ *some milk* _____ ?

   (a.) some milk

   b. a milk

2. The _____ for you.

   a. money isn't

   b. moneys aren't

3. There _____ in the living room.

   a. isn't any furniture

   b. aren't any furnitures

4. We don't have _____. Hurry up!

   a. much time

   b. many times

5. Do you want _____ ?

   a. an apple

   b. some apple

6. Good. There _____ today.

   a. isn't much traffic

   b. aren't many traffics

7. Adam doesn't eat _____.

   a. meat

   b. meats

8. Is there _____ in this store?

   a. any telephone

   b. a telephone

(continued)

9. Do you have _____?

    a. a fruit

    b. any fruit

10. I have a lot of _____ tonight.

    a. homework

    b. homeworks

11. The students need _____.

    a. an information

    b. some information

5 | A AND *THE*

Complete the conversations. Use **a** *or* **the**.

1. **A:** Why don't we go to ___*the*___ Chinese restaurant on Water Street?

    B: OK. I hear ___*the*___ food there is really good.

2. **A:** Can I help you?

    B: Yes, I'd like _____ cup of hot chocolate, please.

3. **A:** Where are your kids?

    B: They're in _____ house.

4. **A:** Are you busy?

    B: Not really. I'm just looking for something on _____ Internet.

5. **A:** Do you have _____ digital camera?

    B: Yes, I do, but it's pretty old.

6. **A:** What is _____ name of her dog?

    B: I can't remember. It's _____ strange name.

7. **A:** How was _____ party at Dan's place?

    B: It was OK. _____ music was good, and I met some new people.

8. **A:** Does Paula have _____ job?

    B: Yeah. She's working as _____ receptionist at _____ publishing company.

6 | SOME, ANY, AND A

Jack went shopping. He didn't buy everything on his shopping list, but he crossed out the things he bought. Write sentences about what he did and didn't buy. Use **some**, **any**, *or* **a**.

> ## Shopping List
>
> ~~bananas~~ toothbrush
>
> cheese ~~potatoes~~
>
> ~~orange juice~~ lettuce
>
> lemons carrots
>
> ~~newspaper~~ ~~butter~~
>
> bread ~~milk~~
>
> onions ~~eggs~~

1. He bought some bananas.

2. He didn't buy any cheese.

3.

4.

5.

6.

7.

8.

9.

10.

11.

12.

13.

14.

7 | COUNT AND NON-COUNT NOUN QUANTIFIERS

Write true sentences. Choose words from each column.

I have	a lot of a little a few	cheese in my pocket food in my refrigerator money in my pocket books next to my bed shirts in my closet
I don't have	much many any	friends free time children work to do today questions for my teacher jewelry medicine in my bathroom problems with my English grammar photographs in my wallet ice cream at home

1. *I don't have any cheese in my pocket.* _____

2. _____

3. _____

4. _____

5. _____

6. _____

7. _____

8. _____

9. _____

10. _____

The Simple Present and Present Progressive; Adverbs and Expressions of Frequency

1 | THE SIMPLE PRESENT AND ADVERBS OF FREQUENCY

Put a check (✓) next to the sentences that are true for you.

_____ 1. I sometimes talk on the phone in the evening.

_____ 2. I always do chores on the weekend.

_____ 3. My friends never sleep at my home.

_____ 4. My English teacher almost always gives me homework.

_____ 5. I don't often cook.

_____ 6. I usually drink coffee in the morning.

_____ 7. I am frequently busy on the weekend.

_____ 8. My classmates rarely ask me for help in class.

_____ 9. It almost never snows in my hometown.

_____10. My home is usually neat and clean.

2 | THE SIMPLE PRESENT AND ADVERBS OF FREQUENCY

Underline the correct adverbs or expressions of frequency. Then write sentences.

1. The doctor says, "I go to the hospital."

   (rarely, <u>usually</u>)   *I usually go to the hospital.*

2. The police officer says, "I arrest people."

   (<u>sometimes</u>, never)   *I sometimes arrest people.*

3. The football player says, "I practice in the middle of the night."

   (always, rarely)   _____

4. The salesperson says, "I fight with customers."

   (always, seldom)   _____

5. The taxi driver says, "I drive at night."

   (never, often) _____

6. The pharmacist says, "I'm careful."

   (always, rarely) _____

7. The mechanic says, "I find the problem with the car."

   (almost always, seldom) _____

8. The chef says, "I put lemon in milk."

   (never, often) _____

9. The factory worker says, "I'm bored."

   (never, once in a while) _____

10. The nurse says, "The hospital is open."

    (every day, frequently) _____

11. The firefighter says, "I wear a suit and tie to work."

    (every day, almost never) _____

12. The flight attendant says, "We're away from home for three or four days."

    (frequently, never) _____

3 | QUESTIONS WITH *HOW OFTEN*

Write questions. Use **how often**. *Then answer the questions. Use the information in the chart.*

	SWIM	PLAY BASKETBALL	DO EXERCISES	JOG
Barbara	three times a week	never	every day	rarely
Donna	once in a while	frequently	four times a week	five days a week
David	never	almost every day	every morning	rarely
Ed	once or twice a week	never	never	often
George	once or twice a week	almost every day	almost every day	almost never

1. (Barbara / do exercises)

How often does Barbara do exercises?

She does exercises every day.

2. (Donna / play basketball)

_____

_____

3. (David / swim)

_____

_____

4. (Barbara and Ed / play basketball)

_____

_____

5. (Ed / jog)

_____

_____

6. (Barbara / swim)

_____

_____

7. (Barbara and David / jog)

_____

_____

8. (Ed and George / swim)

_____

_____

9. (George and David / play basketball)

_____

_____

(continued)

10. (George / jog)

_____

_____

11. (Donna / jog)

_____

_____

12. (Ed / do exercises)

_____

_____

4 | **THE SIMPLE PRESENT**

Match the occupations with the activities.

___i___ **1.** artists   **a.** bake bread and cake

_____ **2.** bakers   **b.** count money

_____ **3.** bank tellers   **c.** cut meat

_____ **4.** bus drivers   **d.** do experiments

_____ **5.** butchers   **e.** drive buses

_____ **6.** doctors   **f.** examine patients

_____ **7.** gardeners   **g.** feed animals

_____ **8.** mechanics   **h.** fix cars

_____ **9.** newspaper reporters **i.** paint pictures

_____ **10.** scientists   **j.** serve food

_____ **11.** waitresses   **k.** water plants and flowers

_____ **12.** zookeepers   **l.** write articles

5 | THE SIMPLE PRESENT AND THE PRESENT PROGRESSIVE

Complete the sentences. Use the correct form of the verbs in Exercise 4.

1. Scott's a doctor. He _____ *examines patients* _____ every day. Right now he's in his

   office. He ___*'s examining a patient*___ .

2. Marilyn's a bus driver. She _____ five days a week. Right

   now she's at work. She _____ .

3. Larry's a mechanic. Every day he _____ . Right now he's at

   his garage. He _____ .

4. Anne's a waitress. Every day she _____ . Right now she's at

   the restaurant. She _____ .

5. Sandra and Pat are artists. They _____ almost every day.

   Right now they're both at their studios. They _____ .

6. Nicholas and Catherine are scientists. They _____ every

   day. Right now they're in the lab. They _____ .

7. Renée and Cathy are newspaper reporters. They _____

   every afternoon. They're at work right now. They _____ .

8. Arthur's a butcher. He _____ every day. Right now he's at

   his store. He _____ .

9. Linda's a bank teller. She _____ all day long. Right now

   she's at the bank. She _____ .

10. Barry and Fred are bakers. They _____ every morning.

    They're in the kitchen now. They _____ .

11. Ruth's a gardener. She _____ almost every day. Right now

    she's at work. She _____ .

12. Jeffrey's a zookeeper. He _____ two times a day. Right now

    he's in the elephant house. He _____ .

6 | THE SIMPLE PRESENT AND THE PRESENT PROGRESSIVE

Complete the telephone conversation. Use the correct form of the verbs in parentheses.

ALAN: Hi, Marsha. This is Alan. What _____ *are you doing* _____ right now?
                                          1. (you / do)

               _____ anything important?
         2. (you / do)

MARSHA: Oh, hi, Alan. No, I _____ some vegetables for dinner.
                                 3. (cut)

ALAN: _____ dinner at this time every evening?
     4. (you / prepare)

MARSHA: Yeah, usually. We _____ at around 8:00. Why? When
                           5. (eat)

               _____ dinner?
         6. (you / have)

ALAN: Oh, my family and I _____ much earlier, probably because our
                               7. (eat)

   kids _____ to bed by 7:30. In fact, they
            8. (go)

   _____ ready for bed right now.
       9. (get)

MARSHA: Really? Our daughter _____ to bed until 9:30, sometimes even
                10. (not go)

   ten o'clock. _____ to bed so early on the weekends, too?
          11. (your kids / go)

ALAN: No, but they _____ later than 8:30. They
             12. (not stay up)

   _____ at around 6:30 every morning, so they
      13. (get up)

   _____ tired by then. What _____ all
      14. (be)   **15. (your daughter / do)**

   evening? _____ a lot of TV?
       16. (she / watch)

MARSHA: No, she _____ the violin. Actually, she
             17. (practice)

   _____ right now.
     18. (practice)

ALAN: How often _____?
            19. (she / practice)

MARSHA: Every day for at least an hour.

ALAN: You're kidding. _____ well?
          20. (she / play)

MARSHA: Very well. We _____ very proud of her.
          21. (be)

ALAN: I'm sure. Listen, I _____ on a report for the office, and there
             22. (work)

   _____ a problem. _____ a couple of
      23. (be)   **24. (you / have)**

   minutes to talk to me about it?

MARSHA: Sure.

Non-Action Verbs

1 | ACTION VERBS AND NON-ACTION VERBS

Underline the verb in each sentence. Then write **action verb** *or* **non-action verb***.*

1. I <u>love</u> to travel.   _____non-action verb_____

2. Does it <u>rain</u> a lot in San Francisco?   _____action verb_____

3. All the hotels have swimming pools.   _____

4. Hotel guests have meals in their rooms.   _____

5. We don't know much about the place.   _____

6. Why are you packing the suitcases now?   _____

7. You need a passport.   _____

8. I'm writing a postcard to my parents.   _____

9. Steve flies to California every month.   _____

10. Do you send e-mails home every day?   _____

11. The food looks good.   _____

12. He looks at the guidebook 10 times a day. _____

13. Do we owe any money?   _____

14. Many tourists visit Paris every year.   _____

2 | THE SIMPLE PRESENT AND THE PRESENT PROGRESSIVE

Complete the sentences. Circle the correct answers and write them on the lines.

1. I _____have_____ 10 dollars. The money's in my bag.

   a. have   **b.** 'm having

2. We _____ help. Let's ask the teacher.

   a. need   **b.** 're needing

3. I'm busy. I _____ on the phone.

   a. talk   **b.** 'm talking

4. She _____ it. Explain it to her again.

   a. doesn't understand   **b.** isn't understanding

5. Pedro _____ his family. That's why he's sad.

   a. misses   **b.** 's missing

6. You _____ in the right place. Look over there!

   a. don't look   **b.** aren't looking

7. There's a problem, but I _____ the answer.

   a. don't know   **b.** 'm not knowing

8. I _____. Don't talk to me!

   a. think   **b.** 'm thinking

9. That shirt _____ good. Buy it!

   a. looks   **b.** 's looking

10. _____ that guy is nice?

    a. Do you think   **b.** Are you thinking

11. There's a car outside. _____ to you?

    a. Does it belong   **b.** Is it belonging

12. The little boy is unhappy. That's why he _____.

    a. cries   **b.** 's crying

13. Let's stay. I _____ a good time.

   a. have   **b.** 'm having

14. That music _____ terrible. Turn it off!

   a. sounds   **b.** 's sounding

3 | THE SIMPLE PRESENT AND THE PRESENT PROGRESSIVE

Complete the conversation. Write the correct form of the verbs in parentheses. Use contractions if possible.

A: What _____*do you want*_____ to do now?
   1. (you / want)

B: I _____. _____ to go to the movies?
   2. (not care)   **3. (you / want)**

A: What _____?
   4. (play)

B: I _____. I _____ a newspaper.
   5. (not know)   **6. (not have)**

A: Well, let's go for a walk and get one.

B: But it _____.
   7. (rain)

A: So what? I _____ an umbrella.
   8. (have)

B: But I _____ one.
   9. (not have)

A: Well, take mine. I _____ it. I _____ the rain.
   10. (not need)   **11. (like)**

B: OK.

A: Maybe Alex _____ to come with us.
   12. (want)

B: I _____ so. He _____ a lot of homework
   13. (not think)   **14. (have)**

   tonight. He _____ it right now.
   15. (do)

A: But I _____ his voice. He _____ on the
   16. (hear)   **17. (talk)**

   phone.

B: He _____ to a classmate. There's something he
   18. (talk)

   _____, and he _____ some help.
   19. (not understand)   **20. (get)**

A: How _____?
   21. (you / know)

B: I _____ everything.
   22. (know)

A: Well, you _____ what's playing at the movies. So let's go!
   23. (not know)

UNIT 28 Gerunds and Infinitives

1 | VERBS

Match the sentences with the speakers.

_h_ **1.** I keep telling Ms. Fox that she needs rest.

_____ **2.** I enjoy fixing things.

_____ **3.** I don't like cleaning all the time.

_____ **4.** All of you need to study more.

_____ **5.** We intend to win.

_____ **6.** Do you want to order something to drink?

_____ **7.** I hope to speak English perfectly one day.

_____ **8.** I avoid playing the piano late at night.

_____ **9.** I prefer working in the movies to working in television.

a. an English-language student

b. an athlete

c. a waiter

d. an actor

e. a musician

f. a maid

g. a mechanic

h. a doctor

i. a teacher

2 | INFINITIVES AND GERUNDS

*Make sentences with **love**, **like**, and **hate**. Use an infinitive or gerund.*

☺ = **love**   ☺ = **like**   ☹ = **hate**

1. Tom—☺—meet new people   *Tom likes meeting new people.*

2. Terry—☹—travel   _____

3. Marsha—☺—take photographs   _____

4. Elena—☺—write poems   _____

5. Steve—☺—be on an airplane   _____

6. Dana—☺—speak other languages   _____

7. Rena—☹—work in an office   _____

8. Leo—☺—learn new things   _____

124

3 | VERBS PLUS INFINITIVES AND GERUNDS

Complete the sentences. Write the correct form of the verbs in the box.

be	help	receive	study	do
~~buy~~	move	relax	swim	talk

1. **A:** Why are you going to the store?

   B: I want _____ *to buy* _____ some fruit.

2. **A:** Why do you go to the swimming pool on Sunday mornings?

   B: I prefer _____ on Sundays. It's quiet then.

3. **A:** Why are you angry with your roommate?

   B: She never wants _____ with the housework.

4. **A:** Why are you closing the door?

   B: I need _____ to you in private.

5. **A:** Why are Gina and Louis looking for an apartment?

   B: They want _____.

6. **A:** Why are they going to the airport so late?

   B: They do not need _____ at the airport until the evening.

7. **A:** Why do you write so many letters?

   B: Because we like _____ them.

8. **A:** Why do you go to the library after class every day?

   B: I prefer _____ my homework there.

9. **A:** Why do you and your wife always stay home on Sundays?

   B: We like _____.

10. **A:** Why are you putting your books away?

    B: Because I finished _____.

29 Review of the Simple Past

1 | AFFIRMATIVE AND NEGATIVE STATEMENTS WITH THE SIMPLE PAST

Complete the sentences. Use the affirmative or negative form of the verb in parentheses.

1. Ana ____*didn't get*____ out
   (get)
   of bed at six o'clock yesterday.

2. She _____
   (make)
   breakfast.

3. She _____ for
   (leave)
   class at half past eight.

4. She and her classmates

   _____ all tired.
   (be)

5. She _____
(have)
lunch alone.

6. In the afternoon she

_____ golf.
(play)

7. She _____
(buy)
some dog food.

8. She _____
(eat)
dinner with Stacy.

9. After dinner she and Boots

_____ TV.
(watch)

2 | *YES / NO* QUESTIONS AND SHORT ANSWERS WITH THE SIMPLE PAST

Answer the questions. Use short answers.

1. Did you use this book last year? _No, I didn't._ _____

2. Were your parents born in New York? _____

3. Did you buy anything yesterday? _____

4. Was your father a good student? _____

5. Was it cold yesterday? _____

6. Did you take a shower yesterday? _____

7. Were you born in a hospital? _____

8. Did your parents get married five years ago? _____

9. Did you and a friend go to the movies last night? _____

10. Was the last grammar exercise easy? _____

11. Did your English teacher give you a test last week? _____

12. Were you absent from your last English class? _____

3 | *YES / NO* QUESTIONS AND ANSWERS WITH THE PAST OF *BE*

*Write questions and answers. Use the past of **be**.*

1. A: _____Was George Washington a soldier?_____ (George Washington / a soldier)

   B: _____Yes, he was a soldier and president._____ (yes / he / a soldier and president)

2. A: _____ (you / good at history in school)

   B: _____ (yes / it / my favorite subject)

3. A: _____ (your history books / interesting)

   B: _____ (they / okay)

4. A: _____ (you / a talkative child)

   B: _____ (no / I / very quiet)

5. A: _____ (your parents / born in the United States)

   B: _____ (no / they / born in Colombia)

6. **A:** _____ (your mother / born in 1942)

   B: _____ (yes / she / born in May 1942)

7. **A:** _____ (Michael Jordan / a great baseball player)

   B: _____ (no / he / a great basketball player)

8. **A:** _____ (the movie about Ray Charles / good)

   B: _____ (yes / the actor / outstanding)

4 | *WH-* QUESTIONS IN THE SIMPLE PAST

Complete the conversations. Circle the correct questions and write them on the lines.

1. **A:** I was absent yesterday.

   B: _What was wrong?_ _____

      a. Who was absent?   **b.** What was wrong?

   A: I was ill.

2. **A:** We had dinner at the new Mexican restaurant.

   B: _____

      a. How was the food?   **b.** Did you like the food?

   A: Yes. It was very good.

3. **A:** You forgot Cathy's birthday.

   B: _____

      a. When was it?   **b.** Where was she?

   A: Last Thursday.

4. **A:** I went to bed at eight o'clock last night.

   B: _____

      a. What did you do?   **b.** Why were you so tired?

   A: I don't know. I didn't feel very well.

5. **A:** You missed a great party.

   B: _____

      a. Who was there?   **b.** How was the party?

   A: People from our class and their friends.

(continued)

6. **A:** I found your keys.

   B: _____

       a. Where did you find them?   **b.** Why were they there?

   A: Under the desk.

7. **A:** I got everything right on the test.

   B: _____

       a. Really? Where were the answers to the first and third questions?

       b. Really? What were the answers to the first and third questions?

   A: The answer to the first was C, and D was the answer to the third.

8. **A:** We were on vacation for two weeks.

   B: _____

       a. Where did you go?   **b.** How was it?

   A: It was great.

9. **A:** We had a great time in Hong Kong.

   B: _____

       a. Who were you with?   **b.** When did you go there?

   A: We were there about two years ago.

10. **A:** I went to a great movie with Andrea last night.

   B: _____

       a. Why didn't you call me and see if I wanted to go?

       b. Why did you go with Andrea and not me?

   A: I did, but you weren't home.

5 | WH- QUESTIONS IN THE SIMPLE PAST

Complete the questions. Use **was**, **were**, *or* **did**. *Then match the questions and answers.*

<u> e </u> **1.** Where <u> *did* </u> you go on vacation?   **a.** My friend Ginny.

_____ **2.** When _____ the flight from New York?   **b.** It was fine, but it rained a few times.

_____ **3.** What _____ you see?   **c.** By plane and bus.

_____ **4.** How _____ the weather?   **d.** Istanbul.

_____ **5.** Where _____ you stay?   **e.** Turkey.

_____ **6.** How _____ you travel around Turkey?   **f.** I always wanted to go to Turkey.

_____ **7.** Who _____ with you?   **g.** At different hotels.

_____ **8.** When _____ your vacation?   **h.** On May 10th.

_____ **9.** How _____ the restaurants?   **i.** Many interesting things.

_____ **10.** Why _____ you go there?   **j.** Some people in the hotels.

_____ **11.** Who _____ you meet?   **k.** Great—Turkish food is delicious.

_____ **12.** What _____ your favorite place?   **l.** In May.

6 | WH- QUESTIONS WITH THE PAST OF *BE*

Complete the conversations. Write correct questions.

1. A: Did you pay a lot of money for those sunglasses?

  B: No, they were on sale.

  A: When <u>*were they on sale*</u> ?

  B: Last week.

2. A: I tried to call you last night.

  B: I wasn't home.

  A: Where _____ ?

  B: At a friend's apartment.

3. A: Did you have your history test yesterday?

  B: No, we had it today.

  A: How _____ ?

  B: It was okay, but I didn't know the answers to two of the questions.

(continued)

4. **A:** Did the kids go swimming?

   B: No, they were afraid.

   A: Why _____?

   B: The water was deep.

5. **A:** Did you go to the basketball game?

   B: Yeah, it was a great game.

   A: What _____?

   B: I don't remember the score, but our team won.

6. **A:** Those are beautiful shoes. Where did you get them?

   B: At a store on Washington Street.

   A: What _____?

   B: I think the name of the store was Dalton's. Or was it Dillon's?

7. **A:** Did your dog have her puppies yet?

   B: She sure did—six of them.

   A: When _____?

   B: They were born a few days ago.

8. **A:** What's new?

   B: The police were here.

   A: Why _____?

   B: Someone called them, but I don't know why.

9. **A:** You were brave to go there alone.

   B: I wasn't alone.

   A: Who _____?

   B: My brother and sister.

10. **A:** Did you ever read this book?

    B: Yes, it was about Eleanor Roosevelt.

    A: Who _____?

    B: She was the wife of President Roosevelt.

Be Going to for the Future

1 | FUTURE TIME MARKERS

Rewrite the sentences. Replace the underlined words with another future time expression.
Use **tonight** *or combine the correct words from each column.*

next	week
this	month
tomorrow	morning
	afternoon
	night
	evening

(It's eight o'clock in the morning on Saturday, April 7th.)

1. Karen is going to take an exam <u>in one hour</u>.

   Karen is going to take an exam this morning.

2. Karen and her boyfriend, Tom, are going to have dinner at a Mexican restaurant <u>in 10 hours</u>.

   _____

3. Karen is going to graduate <u>in one month</u>.

   _____

4. Karen's mother is going to visit <u>in 36 hours</u>.

   _____

5. Karen and her roommate are going to move <u>in one week</u>.

   _____

(continued)

6. Karen is going to see the dentist <u>in seven hours</u>.

_____

7. Karen is going to check her e-mail <u>in 14 hours</u>.

_____

2 | FUTURE TIME MARKERS

Rewrite the sentences. Replace the underlined words with another future time expression.
Use **in**.

(It is two o'clock in the afternoon on Monday, October 13th.)

1. Max is going to attend a meeting <u>at four o'clock this afternoon</u>.

   Max is going to attend a meeting in two hours.

2. Max is going to leave the office <u>at 2:15 this afternoon</u>.

_____

3. Max and Debbie are going to get married <u>on April 13th</u>.

_____

4. Debbie is going to start a new job <u>on October 27th</u>.

_____

5. Debbie is going to take Max to her parents' home <u>on Friday, October 17th</u>.

_____

3 | FUTURE PLANS

What are your plans for tomorrow? Put a check (✔) next to the things you are probably
going to do. Put an **X** next to the things you are definitely not going to do.

_____ **1.** study

_____ **2.** go shopping

_____ **3.** take pictures

_____ **4.** watch TV

_____ **5.** go out with friends

_____ **6.** listen to music

_____ **7.** visit relatives

_____ **8.** talk on the telephone

_____ **9.** take a shower

_____ **10.** check my e-mail

_____ **11.** go skiing

_____ **12.** stay home

4 | AFFIRMATIVE AND NEGATIVE STATEMENTS WITH *BE GOING TO*

Write six true sentences about your plans for tomorrow. Use the information from Exercise 3.

Example:

__✓__ study   __✗__ check my e-mail

I am going to study tomorrow.

I am not going to check my e-mail.

1. _____

2. _____

3. _____

4. _____

5. _____

6. _____

5 | AFFIRMATIVE STATEMENTS WITH *BE GOING TO*

Some people are going out. What are they going to do? Make guesses and write sentences with **be going to***.*

Nora is taking a cell phone and car keys.

1. *She's going to talk on the phone.* _____

2. _____

Jessica and Peter Greblo are taking a suitcase and a camera.

3. _____

4. _____

David is taking a DVD and a textbook.

5. _____

6. _____

6 | NEGATIVE STATEMENTS WITH *BE GOING TO*

Write sentences about the future. Use **not** *and* **be going to**.

1. It's Wednesday morning. Reggie usually plays tennis on Wednesday afternoon, but he has a bad cold.

   _____*He isn't going to play*_____ tennis this afternoon.

2. It's July. Joan usually takes a vacation in August, but she has money problems this year.

   _____ a vacation this August.

3. Mary always takes a shower in the morning, but there's no hot water today.

   _____ a shower this morning.

4. It's 11 o'clock in the morning. The children usually play outside after lunch, but the weather is terrible today.

   _____ outside this afternoon.

5. It's six o'clock. Carl and his wife usually watch television after dinner, but there's nothing good on television.

   _____ television tonight.

6. It's 11 o'clock. I usually eat lunch around noon, but I finished a big breakfast at 10:30.

   _____ lunch at noon today.

7. It's 12 noon. My friend and I like to swim on Saturday afternoons, but my friend went away for the weekend and I'm tired.

   _____ this afternoon.

8. It's nine o'clock in the morning. Dr. Morita usually sees patients at his office every morning, but there's an emergency at the hospital. He can't leave until noon.

   _____ patients at his office this morning.

9. I usually wake up at six o'clock in the morning, but tomorrow is a holiday.

   _____ at six o'clock tomorrow morning.

10. It's 10 o'clock in the morning. The letter carrier usually delivers all the mail by one o'clock, but he started late this morning.

    _____ all the mail by one o'clock today.

7 | *WH-* QUESTIONS WITH *BE GOING TO*

Write questions. Use **be going to**.

1. What / he / make

   What is he going to make?

2. Who / cook / tonight

   _____

3. When / dinner / be / ready

   _____

4. Why / he / cook / so much food

   _____

5. How long / he / need / to cook the dinner

   _____

6. Who / come

   _____

7. How / he / cook / the lamb

   _____

8. Where / all of your guests / sit

   _____

9. What / you / do

   _____

10. How long / your guests / stay

   _____

8 | *WH-* QUESTIONS WITH *BE GOING TO*

Write the correct questions from Exercise 7.

1. **A:** *Who's going to cook tonight?*

   B: My husband.

2. **A:** _____

   B: Soup, salad, lamb, potatoes, some vegetables, and dessert.

(continued)

3. **A:** _____

   B: We're going to have a dinner party.

4. **A:** _____

   B: He's going to roast it in the oven.

5. **A:** _____

   B: About 15 of my relatives.

6. **A:** _____

   B: My husband's fast. Probably two or three hours.

7. **A:** _____

   B: I'm going to wash the dishes.

8. **A:** _____

   B: At around seven o'clock.

9. **A:** _____

   B: They're going to come at 6:00 and probably stay until about 11:00.

10. **A:** _____

    B: My sister's going to bring extra chairs.

9 | PRESENT PROGRESSIVE FOR NOW AND FOR FUTURE

*Underline the verb in each sentence. Write **now** if the speaker is talking about now. Write **future** if the speaker is talking about the future.*

1. Where <u>is</u> he <u>going</u> next week?   *future*

2. Where <u>is</u> he <u>going</u>?   *now*

3. I'm doing my homework.   _____

4. We're not having a meeting on Monday.   _____

5. They're moving in three weeks.   _____

6. Are you having dinner?   _____

7. Are you leaving soon?   _____

8. The children are not sleeping.   _____

9. Where are you going on the weekend?   _____

10. Why is he coming?   _____

10 | PRESENT PROGRESSIVE FOR FUTURE

Roger and Helen are taking a trip to Great Britain. Here is their schedule.
Write sentences. Use the present progressive.

May 8	6:00 P.M.	Meet your group at the airport
	7:30	Fly to London
May 9	6:45 A.M.	Arrive in London
May 9 and 10		Stay at the London Regency Hotel
May 9	2:00 P.M.	Visit Buckingham Palace
	4:30	Have tea at the Ritz Hotel
	7:30	Go to the theater
May 10	9:00 A.M.	Go on a tour of central London
	12:00 P.M.	Eat lunch at a typical English pub
May 11	8:00 A.M.	Leave for Scotland

1. *They are meeting their group at the airport at 6:00 P.M. on May 8.* _____

2. _____

3. _____

4. _____

5. _____

6. _____

7. _____

8. _____

9. _____

10. _____

11 | YES / NO QUESTIONS AND ANSWERS WITH THE PRESENT PROGRESSIVE FOR FUTURE

Write questions. Use the present progressive. Then answer them. Use short answers.

1. you / meet / friends / tomorrow

   Are you meeting friends tomorrow?   _Yes, I am._ (OR *No, I'm not.*)

2. you / go / shopping / this weekend

   _____   _____

3. you / work / next week

   _____   _____

4. your friend / have / a party / next Saturday

   _____   _____

5. your classmates / study / with you / tonight

   _____   _____

6. your neighbor / come / to your place / tomorrow

   _____   _____

7. your parents / move / next year

   _____   _____

8. your classmates / have / dinner together / tomorrow

   _____   _____

9. you and your friends / play / video games / on the weekend

   _____   _____

10. your teacher / make / lunch for you / tomorrow

   _____   _____

12 | *WH-* QUESTIONS AND ANSWERS WITH THE PRESENT PROGRESSIVE FOR FUTURE

Ask Rosemary about her vacation plans. Write questions. Use a word from each column and the present progressive.

Why		stay
When		take
Where		go
Who	you	go with
How long		leave
What		drive
How		get there

1. *Where are you going?*

   To Colorado.

2. _____

   On September 16th.

3. _____

   By car.

4. _____

   Airplane tickets are too expensive.

5. _____

   Two weeks.

6. _____

   Some friends from college.

7. _____

   A tent, sleeping bags, and bikes.

31 *Will* for the Future; Future Time Markers

1 | AFFIRMATIVE STATEMENTS WITH *WILL*

*Complete the conversations. Use **I'll** and the words in the box.*

make you a sandwich	get you some aspirin	~~close the window~~	wash them
turn on the air conditioner	get you some water	help you	drive you

1. **A:** I'm cold.

   B: *I'll close the window.* _____

2. **A:** I'm thirsty.

   B: _____

3. **A:** I can't lift this box.

   B: _____

4. **A:** I need some stamps.

   B: _____

5. **A:** I'm hot.

   B: _____

6. **A:** I'm hungry.

   B: _____

7. **A:** I have a headache.

   B: _____

8. **A:** I'm late for class.

   B: _____

9. **A:** There are dirty dishes in the sink.

   B: _____

2 | CONTRACTIONS WITH *WILL*

Write the sentences with contractions.

1. We will see you tomorrow. *We'll see you tomorrow.*

2. He will be very happy there. _____

3. I will be there early. _____

4. She will not do it. _____

5. It will be hot tomorrow. _____

6. They will not come. _____

7. You will not get the job. _____

3 | *WILL, BE GOING TO,* AND PRESENT PROGRESSIVE FOR FUTURE

Complete the sentences. Circle the correct words and write them on the lines.

1. **A:** What's the weather forecast for tomorrow?

    B: The newspaper says it _____*will snow*_____.

      a. is snowing   **(b.)** will snow

2. **A:** Where are you going with the soap and water?

    B: I _____ wash the car.

      a. am going to   **b.** will

3. **A:** Do you see my umbrella?

    B: Yes, it's over there. I _____ get it for you.

      a. am going to   **b.** will

4. **A:** Why is Myra so happy these days?

    B: She _____ get married.

      a. is going to   **b.** will

5. **A:** Why _____ see that film?

      a. are you going to   **b.** will you

    B: I heard it was good.

6. **A:** The dishwasher isn't working. I'm going to call the repairman.

   B: No, don't. I _____ it.

   a. am fixing   **b.** will fix

7. **A:** I think men _____ dresses in the future.

   a. are wearing   **b.** will wear

   B: You're crazy!

8. **A:** _____ anything this weekend?

   a. Are you doing   **b.** Will you do

   B: I'm not sure yet. Why?

9. **A:** _____ everything by computer in 50 years?

   a. Are people buying   **b.** Will people buy

   B: Maybe.

4 | NEGATIVE STATEMENTS WITH *WILL*

Write negative sentences with the same meaning.

1. The car will be small.

   The car won't be big.

2. I'll leave early.

   _____

3. It'll be cold.

   _____

4. Coffee will cost less.

   _____

5. The dishes will be clean.

   _____

6. We will come after seven o'clock.

   _____

7. Mr. and Mrs. McNamara will buy an old car.

   _____

8. I'll make a few eggs.

_____

9. Valerie will win the game.

_____

10. The parking lot will be empty.

_____

5 | AFFIRMATIVE AND NEGATIVE STATEMENTS AND *YES / NO* AND *WH-* QUESTIONS WITH *WILL*

*A fortune teller is telling Mark about his future. Complete the conversation. Use **will** or **won't** and the words in parentheses.*

FORTUNE TELLER: Your future _____ *will be* _____ a happy one.
                                          1. (be)

MARK: _____ rich?
        2. (I / be)

FORTUNE TELLER: Yes. You _____ a very rich woman.
                          3. (marry)

MARK: Where _____ her?
        4. (I / meet)

FORTUNE TELLER: That I can't tell you, but it _____ love at first sight.
                                              5. (be)

MARK: _____ me forever?
        6. (she / love)

FORTUNE TELLER: Forever.

MARK: When _____?
        7. (we / meet)

FORTUNE TELLER: Soon.

MARK: What about children?

FORTUNE TELLER: You _____ many children—just two, a boy and a girl.
                      8. (not have)

MARK: That's a good number. What else?

FORTUNE TELLER: You _____ famous.
                      9. (be)

MARK: Really? Why _____ famous?
                    10. (I / be)

FORTUNE TELLER: I'm not sure, but it _____ fun for you. People
                                      11. (not be)
_____ you all the time.
12. (bother)

MARK: Oh! I _____ that. _____
            13. (not like)   **14. (our home / have)**
everything?

FORTUNE TELLER: Yes, everything.

(continued)

MARK: Good. Then we _____ it, and people
15. (not leave)

_____ us.
16. (not bother)

FORTUNE TELLER: But then you _____ a prisoner in your own home.
17. (become)

_____ you happy?
18. (that / make)

MARK: Oh, why isn't life perfect?

FORTUNE TELLER: That I cannot tell you.

---

6 | REVIEW OF PRESENT, PAST, AND FUTURE

Complete the sentences. Choose the present, the past, or the future with **will**. *Use the verbs in parentheses.*

Well, here I am on the moon. We _____*arrived*_____ a few hours ago. First, I
1. (arrive)

_____ a walk on the moon. It _____ so strange. Then we
2. (take) 3. (be)

_____ something, but it _____ normal food. Right now we
4. (eat) 5. (be not)

_____. Of course, we _____ and we _____
6. (rest) 7. (not sit) 8. (not lie)

down. This is outer space and people _____ here. And they
9. (not sit)

_____ down here either. We _____ here for three more days.
10. (not lie) 11. (be)

Then we _____ to Earth. It _____ a long trip, but I'm sure it
12. (return) 13. (not be)

_____ fun.
14. (be)

May or *Might* for Possibility

1 | *MAY* and *MIGHT* FOR POSSIBILITY

*Put a check (✔) next to the sentences that are possible where you live. Put an **X** next to the sentences that are not possible. Use the map to help you.*

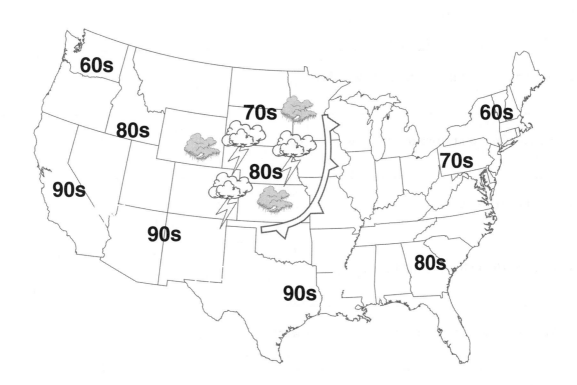

_____ 1. It might rain tomorrow.

_____ 2. It may snow next month.

_____ 3. It may not be sunny tomorrow.

_____ 4. It might be windy next week.

_____ 5. It might be very cold on the weekend.

(continued)

____ **6.** It may be 37 degrees Celsius (98.6°F) next month.

____ **7.** It may be very hot tomorrow.

____ **8.** It might be windy next week.

____ **9.** It might not be nice tomorrow morning.

____ **10.** It might be −5 degrees Celsius (23°F) tonight.

2 | *MAY* AND *MIGHT* FOR POSSIBILITY

Rewrite the sentences. Use **may** *or* **might***.*

1. Maybe it will snow.

　　It may snow. (OR *It might snow.*) _____

2. Perhaps they won't listen to the weather report.

_____

3. Perhaps he won't drive in the snow.

_____

4. Maybe they will stay home.

_____

5. Perhaps she will go to the beach.

_____

6. Maybe we won't ride our bikes in the hot weather.

_____

7. Maybe you will need a hat.

_____

8. Perhaps I won't like the weather there.

_____

9. Maybe the weather report will be wrong.

_____

10. Perhaps the weather will improve.

_____

3 | *WILL* **FOR DEFINITE FUTURE AND** *MAY* **FOR POSSIBILITY**

Complete the sentences. Use **may** *or* **will**.

1. Tomorrow is my birthday. I _____*will*_____ be 25.

2. I'm tall. My children _____*may*_____ be tall, too.

3. I don't know anything about that movie. It _____ not be good.

4. Are you taking a trip to the United States? You _____ need a passport.

   Everybody from Brazil needs one.

5. Don't worry. I _____ do it. I promise.

6. Ask about the price. It _____ be expensive.

7. The supermarket _____ sell flowers, but I'm not sure.

8. There's someone at the door. I _____ open it.

9. The sun _____ rise tomorrow.

10. The food _____ be ready. I'm going to look.

4 | **AFFIRMATIVE AND NEGATIVE STATEMENTS WITH** *MAY* **AND** *MIGHT*

Complete the sentences. Use **may (not)** *or* **might (not)** *and the words in the box.*

bite	close	get lost	have an accident	~~pass~~
break	~~fall~~	get sick	live	win

1. Janet is worried about her little boy. He's climbing a tree.

   He _may fall. (OR *might fall.*)_____

2. Jimmy has a test today, and he didn't study.

   He _may not pass. (OR *might not pass.*)_____

3. Lynn is driving fast.

   She _____

4. Wrap those glasses carefully.

   They _____

(continued)

5. Mark Muller is one of the top tennis players in the world, but he isn't playing well today.

He _____

6. Don't lose these directions. It's difficult to find my house.

You _____

7. The woman's injuries are very bad.

She _____

8. Don't go near that animal.

It _____

9. Don't go outside with wet hair. It's cold.

You _____

10. That store never has many customers.

It _____

Questions with *Any* / *Some* / *How Much* / *How Many;* Quantity Expressions

---

1 | **CONTAINERS AND NON-COUNT NOUNS**

Match the containers and non-count nouns.

<u> b </u>   **1.** a can of

a. lettuce

_____   **2.** a carton of

b. soda

_____   **3.** a head of

c. bread

_____   **4.** a loaf of

d. milk

Do the same with these words.

_____   **5.** a bottle of

e. cheese

_____   **6.** a box of

f. gum

_____   **7.** a pack of

g. juice

_____   **8.** a piece of

h. cereal

Do the same with these words, too.

_____ **9.** a bar of   **i.** toothpaste

_____ **10.** a jar of   **j.** toilet paper

_____ **11.** a roll of   **k.** jam

_____ **12.** a tube of   **l.** soap

---

2 | **QUESTIONS WITH *HOW MUCH* AND *HOW MANY* AND CONTAINERS**

Look at Tina's cash register receipt and answer the questions.

```
6 Soda              $2.99
1 Bread             $1.95
1 milk              $1.99
2 Lettuce           $3.98
3 Apple juice       $8.97
1 Cereal            $3.59
4 Toilet paper      $1.99
3 Soap              $2.45
1 Toothpaste        $2.50
2 Jam               $5.00

            TOTAL   $35.41
```

1. How much soda did she buy?

_____*Six cans.*_____

2. How many loaves of bread did she buy?

_____*One / One loaf.*_____

3. How much milk did she buy?

_____

4. How much lettuce did she buy?

_____

5. How many bottles of apple juice did she buy?

_____

6. How many boxes of cereal did she buy?

_____

7. How much toilet paper did she buy?

_____

8. How much soap did she buy?

_____

9. How much toothpaste did she buy?

_____

10. How many jars of jam did she buy?

_____

3 | *YES / NO* QUESTIONS WITH COUNT AND NON-COUNT NOUNS

Write questions. Use **a**, **an**, *or* **any**. *Then answer the questions with short answers.*

1. book / on your bed

   Is there a book on your bed?   Yes, there is. (OR: No, there isn't.)

2. cheese / in your refrigerator

   Is there any cheese in your refrigerator?   Yes, there is. (OR: No, there isn't.)

3. shoes / under your bed

   Are there any shoes under your bed?   Yes, there are. (OR: No, there aren't.)

4. cell phone / in your pocket

   _____   _____

5. money / in your wallet

   _____   _____

6. CDs / in your bedroom

   _____   _____

7. flowers / in your kitchen

   _____   _____

8. cars / on your street

   _____   _____

9. computer / in your bedroom

   _____   _____

10. DVD player / in your home

    _____   _____

11. remote control / next to your bed

    _____   _____

12. jewelry / in your home

    _____   _____

13. food / on your kitchen table

    _____   _____

14. furniture / in your living room

    _____   _____

4 | QUESTIONS WITH *HOW MUCH* AND *HOW MANY*

Complete the conversation. Write questions using **how much** *or* **how many**.

A: Are you going to the store?

B: Yes, why?

A: I need some things. I need some cheese.

B: *How much cheese do you need?*
1.

A: About a pound. And I want some eggs.

B: *How many eggs do you want?*
2.

A: A dozen. I also need some flour.

B: _____
3.

A: One pound, I think.

B: Do you want any sugar?

A: No, I have sugar.

B: _____
4.

A: I have a few cups, at least. But I want some bananas.

B: _____
5.

A: Five or six. I want some oranges, too.

B: _____
6.

A: A few. Oh, and I need some cereal.

B: _____
7.

A: Just one box. I also need some potatoes.

B: _____
8.

A: Get about 10. Oh, one more thing. I want some milk.

B: _____
9.

A: Half a gallon. Oh, don't forget to get some flowers. I want roses.

B: _____
10.

A: Half a dozen.

B: Is that it? Are you sure you don't want any cookies?

A: No, I have enough cookies.

B: _____

11.

A: Two dozen. Here, let me give you some money.

B: I have money.

A: _____

12.

B: About $20.

A: Here. Take another 20.

5 | ENOUGH

Complete the sentences. Use **is / is not enough** *and a word from the box.*

exercise	fruit	sleep	spinach	water

1. She exercises 60 minutes every day. That _is enough exercise. (OR is not enough exercise.)_

2. He exercises two times every week. That _____

3. They eat four servings of fruit every day. That _____

4. She eats two servings of spinach every day. That _____

5. He drinks four glasses of water every day. That _____

6. They sleep six hours every day. That _____

1 | TOO

*Complete the sentences. Use **too** and a word in the box.*

big	crowded	expensive	heavy	hot	old	~~small~~	young

1. The jeans are nice, but I wear a size 36. They're a size 34.

   They're _____*too small*_____.

2. Let's go to another restaurant. Look at all the people in this restaurant.

   It's _____.

3. The price for children under 10 is five dollars. Your son can't pay five dollars. He's 12.

   He's _____.

4. It's 38 degrees Celsius (100.4°F) outside. I don't want to go for a walk.

   It's _____.

5. We can only take suitcases that are 20 kilos or less. Your suitcase is 40 kilos.

   It's _____.

6. I like the watch, but I never spend more than $100 on a watch. It costs $300.

   It's _____.

7. I can't wear these shoes. I wear a size 7, and they're a size 9.

   They're _____.

8. You're only 14 years old. You can't stay at your friend's party until midnight.

   You're _____.

2 | TOO MUCH, TOO MANY, AND *NOT ENOUGH*

Write sentences about the pictures. Use **too much**, **too many**, *or* **not enough** *and the words in the box.*

air	birds	days	furniture	~~people~~	toothpaste
batteries	chairs	food	numbers	shampoo	water

1.

There are too many people

in the boat.

2.

3.

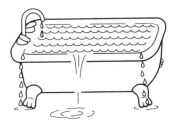

4.

5.

6.

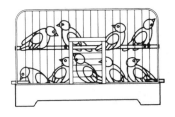

7.

8.

9.

(continued)

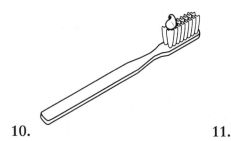

10.

11.

12.

_____   _____   _____

_____   _____   _____

3 | *TOO LITTLE* AND *TOO FEW*

Rewrite the sentences. Use **too little** *or* **too few**.

1. We don't have enough chairs.

   We have too few chairs.

2. There isn't enough salt in this soup.

   There's too little salt in this soup.

3. There weren't enough people for two teams.

   _____

4. We didn't have enough paper for everyone in the class.

   _____

5. There wasn't enough food for 15 people.

   _____

6. You don't have enough information.

   _____

7. There aren't enough bedrooms in that apartment.

   _____

8. We didn't have enough time for the test.

   _____

9. There aren't enough bananas for a banana cake.

   _____

10. There aren't enough sales clerks at that store.

   _____

4 | REVIEW OF QUANTIFIERS

Complete the sentences. Circle the correct answers and write them on the lines.

1. What did the student say to the teacher?

   "I didn't finish the homework. I _____*didn't have enough*_____ time."

   a. had too much

   (b.) didn't have enough

2. What did the driver say to the passenger?

   "We _____ gas. We need to go to the gas station."

   a. have too much

   b. don't have enough

3. What did the passenger say to the driver?

   "There _____ cars. Let's go to another parking lot."

   a. are too many

   b. aren't enough

4. What did the cashier say to the child?

   "I'm sorry. You have _____ money. Go home and get some more."

   a. too much

   b. too little

5. Ted and Niki wanted to see a movie, but there was a long line for tickets. What did Ted say?

   "There are _____ people. Let's see another movie."

   a. too many

   b. too few

6. What did the doctor say to the patient?

   "You said you're on a diet, but you lost only one pound last month. That

   _____ weight."

   a. is too much

   b. isn't enough

(continued)

7. What did the photography teacher say to the student?

   "This picture is dark. You had _____ light."

   a. too much

   b. too little

8. What did Mitchell's mother say to him?

   "You ate _____ fruit. That's why you have a stomachache."

   a. too much

   b. too little

9. What did the customer say to the waitress?

   "There are _____ forks on the table for six people. Please bring some

   more."

   a. too many

   b. too few

10. What did Debbie say to her roommate?

    "You bought _____ juice. There's no place to put all these bottles."

    a. too much

    b. too little

Possessives

1 | POSSESSIVE ADJECTIVES AND POSSESSIVE PRONOUNS

Write **correct** *if the sentence is correct. Write* **car** *in the sentences where a noun is necessary.*

1. Your is not working. *Your car is not working.*

2. Mine is not working. *correct*

3. Is this yours? _____

4. Ours is over there. _____

5. Please bring me my. _____

6. Where is her? _____

7. Give me hers, please. _____

8. Theirs is on Park Street. _____

9. We need our. _____

10. Their is expensive. _____

11. I like mine a lot. _____

12. Why do you want your? _____

2 | POSSESSIVE PRONOUNS

Complete the sentences. Use **mine**, **yours**, **his**, **hers**, **ours**, *or* **theirs**.

1. That is not her bicycle. _____ *Hers* _____ is blue.

2. That's not my jacket. _____ is gray.

3. **A:** Is that his classroom?

   B: No, _____ is on the fifth floor.

(continued)

4. A: Is that our suitcase?

    B: No, _____ is not light brown. We have a dark brown suitcase.

5. These are not your shoes. _____ are under the bed.

6. A: Is that their house?

    B: No, _____ is on Middle Street.

7. A: Are those your son's sneakers?

    B: No, _____ are a size 12.

8. A: Is that Ms. Gilman's office?

    B: No, _____ is in the next building.

9. These are not Yuri and Natasha's test papers. _____ are on my desk.

10. My roommate and I have a sofa like that one, but _____ is a little bigger.

3 | POSSESSIVE ADJECTIVES AND POSSESSIVE PRONOUNS

Complete the conversations. Use the correct possessive adjective or possessive pronoun.

1. A: This is not _____ *my* _____ coat.

    B: Where's _____ *yours* _____?

    A: In the closet.

2. A: That's _____ ball. Give it to me!

    B: It's not _____. It's _____. It's a birthday present from my

    brother.

3. A: Whose scarf is this?

    B: It's Nancy's.

    A: Are you sure it's _____? This scarf is green, and she rarely wears green.

    B: I'm sure it's _____.

4. A: We're so happy with _____ new car. We love it.

    B: You're lucky. We don't like _____ at all.

5. **A:** Do you know Bonnie and Tony Gray? _____ son is on the football team.

   B: We know them, but we don't know _____ son. Our son is on the middle

   school team, but _____ is on the high school team.

6. **A:** Is this your husband's hat?

   B: Yes, it is.

   A: How do you know it's _____?

   B: Because all of _____ hats have his name inside.

4 | REVIEW OF PRONOUNS AND POSSESSIVES

Complete the sentences. Choose the correct words in parentheses. (Use only three of the words.)

1. (I, me, mine, my)

   The laptop is __*mine*__. __*My*__ parents bought it for __*me*__ last year.

2. (our, ours, us, we)

   Hello. _____ last name is Todd. _____ called an hour ago. Do you have a table for

   _____?

3. (our, ours, us, we)

   Excuse me. _____ don't want to bother you, but those seats are _____. Here are

   _____ tickets.

4. (I, me, my, mine)

   Please introduce _____ to the man at the table. He's _____ neighbor, but _____

   don't know him.

5. (he, him, his, his)

   That hat belongs to my brother. _____ name is in it. The jacket is _____ too. Please

   give the hat and jacket to _____.

   (continued)

6. (you, you, your, yours)

Those aren't _____ keys. _____ are on the table. _____ always forget something.

7. (it, it, it's, its)

I rarely read that magazine. _____ is hard to find in my neighborhood, and I don't like

_____ very much. _____ articles are often long and boring.

8. (their, theirs, them, they)

The car is _____ father's. It isn't _____. He often gives the car to _____ on the

weekend.

9. (her, her, hers, she)

Do you know _____? _____ is my neighbor. The dog is _____.

Can or May for Permission

1 | *CAN* OR *MAY* IN STATEMENTS

Complete the sentences. Circle the correct answers and write them on the lines.

1. The doctor says, "You ___*can*___ call me at night. It's not a problem.

   (a.) can

   b. can't

2. The teacher says, "You _____ use your cell phone in class. Do not bring your phone to class."

   a. can

   b. can't

3. Sam's father says, "You _____ drive my car. You're too young."

   a. may

   b. may not

4. The police officer says, "You _____ park in front of a bus stop. Move your car."

   a. can

   b. can't

5. The nurse says, "You _____ go into the room now. Dorothy is waiting for you."

   a. may

   b. may not

6. The store manager says, "You _____ smoke in the store. It's against the law."

   a. can

   b. can't

(continued)

7. Karen's mother says, "You _____ go to the movies, but be home before eleven o'clock."

    a. can

    b. can't

8. The office manager says, "You _____ leave at four o'clock, but not before then."

    a. may

    b. may not

2 | *MAY* AND *CAN* FOR POLITE REQUESTS

Complete the requests. Use the words in the box.

bring my boyfriend	~~open the window~~	sit here
come in	pay by credit card	speak to the doctor

1. **A:** I'm cold. May *I open the window* _____?

    B: Yes, you may.

2. **A:** The total is $109.50.

    B: Can _____?

    A: Sure.

3. **A:** Mark, is that you at the door?

    B: Yes, it is. May _____?

    A: Of course.

4. **A:** Hello. Dr. Asbury's office. Connie speaking.

    B: Hello. This is Chris Nelson. Can _____?

    A: I'm sorry, but he's with a patient.

5. **A:** Hello.

    B: Hello. May _____?

    A: Sure. The seat's free.

6. **A:** Please come to my party next Saturday.

    B: Can _____?

    A: Of course.

3 | *MAY AND CAN* FOR POLITE REQUESTS

Make polite requests. Use **may I** *or* **can I**.

1. You have a doctor's appointment at four o'clock. You want to leave early because class ends at four o'clock. Ask your teacher.

   Can I leave class early? (OR May I leave class early?)

2. You're in a friend's room. You're hot and you want to open the window. Ask your friend.

   _____

3. You're in an office. You want to use the telephone on the secretary's desk. Ask the secretary.

   _____

4. Your classmate has a car, but you don't have one. It's raining, and you want to get a ride. Ask your classmate.

   _____

5. You made a mistake. You don't have an eraser, but your classmate has an eraser. Ask your classmate.

   _____

6. You're at your neighbor's house. You want to have a drink of water. Ask your neighbor.

   _____

7. You have a question about something in your grammar book. Ask your teacher.

   _____

8. You're at a restaurant. You want to sit at the empty table in the corner. Ask the waiter.

   _____

37 Requests, Desires, and Offers: *Would You Please. . . .?*, *I'd Like. . . ., Would You Like. . . .?*

1 | AFFIRMATIVE STATEMENTS AND QUESTIONS WITH *WOULD LIKE*

Read each conversation. Then answer the question.

Conversation A

A: Can I help you?

B: Yes, I'd like two tickets to Pittsburgh.

A: Would you like one-way or round-trip?

B: Round-trip, please.

A: That's $70.

B: Here you are. What time is the next bus?

A: At 9:30.

B: Thank you.

1. Where does Conversation A take place? _____

Conversation B

A: Sir, would you like chicken or fish?

B: Chicken, please.

A: And what would you like to drink?

B: Just some water, please.

A: And your wife?

B: She doesn't want anything. She doesn't like airplane food.

2. Where does Conversation B take place? _____

Conversation C

A: Where would you like to sit?

B: These seats are fine. I don't want to sit too close to the screen.

A: Would you like some popcorn?

B: No, but I'd like something to drink. But hurry! The movie's going to start.

3. Where does Conversation C take place? _____

2 | AFFIRMATIVE STATEMENTS AND *YES / NO* QUESTIONS WITH *WOULD LIKE*

Rewrite the sentences. Use **would like***.*

1. I want two tickets for *Heartless*, please.

   I would like two tickets for Heartless, please.

2. Do you want to go to the movies tonight?

   Would you like to go to the movies tonight?

3. The teacher wants to see you.

   _____

4. Do the children want hamburgers or hot dogs?

   _____

5. Do you want to check your e-mail on my computer?

   _____

6. Does Paul want to come to the party?

   _____

7. My husband wants rice with his fish.

   _____

8. Neil and Jane want a bigger apartment.

   _____

9. Do you want to have a cup of coffee with me?

   _____

10. We want to go home now.

    _____

3 | STATEMENTS AND QUESTIONS WITH *WOULD LIKE*

Complete the conversation. Use the words in parentheses.

DAVE: Hi, Ellen. Come on in.

ELLEN: Hi, Dave. Thanks.

DAVE: _____*Would you like*_____ some coffee?
              1. (you / like)

(continued)

ELLEN: Yes. That sounds good. _____ some help?
2.(you / like)

DAVE: No, it's ready. Here you are.

ELLEN: Thanks.

DAVE: _____ some cookies, too?
3.(you / like)

ELLEN: No, thanks, but I _____ some sugar for my coffee.
4.(like)

DAVE: Oh, sorry. I forgot. Here's the sugar.

ELLEN: Boy, it's cold outside.

DAVE: _____ a sweater?
5.(you / like)

ELLEN: No, I'm okay.

DAVE: So, _____ this evening?
6.(what / you / like / do)

ELLEN: I don't know. _____?
7.(Where / you / like / go)

DAVE: _____ to the movies?
8.(you / like / go)

ELLEN: What's playing?

DAVE: *Forever Love* is at the Rex. _____ that?
9.(you / like / see)

ELLEN: Okay. What time does it start?

DAVE: We can go at six, eight, or ten.

ELLEN: I don't care. _____?
10.(What time / you / like / go)

DAVE: Eight is fine, but I _____ something to eat first.
11.(like / get)

ELLEN: Okay. _____?
12.(Where / you / like / eat)

DAVE: How about John's Pizzeria?

ELLEN: That sounds good.

4 | WOULD, COULD, AND CAN FOR POLITE REQUESTS

Write correct questions. Use **please** *with* **would you, could you,** *or* **can you**.

1. Ask a stranger on the bus to tell you the time.

   Would you please tell me the time? (OR *Could you please tell me the time?*)

2. Ask a desk clerk at a hotel to give you the key to your room.

   _____

3. Ask your teacher to explain the meaning of the word *grateful*.

_____

4. Ask a cashier to give you change for a dollar.

_____

5. Ask a stranger to take a picture of you and your friends.

_____

6. Ask a taxi driver to take you to the airport.

_____

7. Ask a neighbor to help you with your suitcases.

_____

8. Ask a sales clerk to show you the brown shoes in the window.

_____

9. Ask the person in front of you at a basketball game to sit down.

_____

5 | RESPONSES

Complete the conversations. Circle the correct answers and write them on the lines.

1. A: Would you like some cream in your coffee?

   B: _No, thank you._

   a. No, I wouldn't.

   b. No, thank you.

2. A: Would you like to have dinner with us tonight?

   B: _____

   a. Yes, I would. Thank you.

   b. I do.

3. A: Could you move your bag, please?

   B: _____

   a. Sure.

   b. I could.

(continued)

4. **A:** Would you help me?

   B: _____

   a. Yes, thanks.

   b. Of course.

5. **A:** Can you give me a lift to the office?

   B: _____

   a. I'm sorry, I can't. My car's not working.

   b. No, I don't.

6. **A:** Would you like something to drink?

   B: _____

   a. Yes, I would. Thanks.

   b. Yes, I would like.

Advice: *Should, Shouldn't, Ought to, Had Better, and Had Better Not*

1 | AFFIRMATIVE AND NEGATIVE STATEMENTS WITH *SHOULD*

*Complete the sentences. Use **should** or **shouldn't**.*

1. Children _____*shouldn't*_____ play with matches.

2. Children _____ watch television all day long.

3. Children _____ listen to their parents.

4. Children _____ eat a lot of candy.

5. Children _____ play in the street.

6. Teenagers _____ pay attention in school.

7. Teenagers _____ keep their bedrooms neat.

8. Teenagers _____ stay out all night with their friends.

9. Adults _____ exercise at least twice a week.

10. Adults _____ drink 10 cups of coffee a day.

2 | AFFIRMATIVE STATEMENTS WITH *OUGHT TO*

*Rewrite the sentences. Use **ought to**.*

1. You should read this book about cultural differences.

   You ought to read this book about cultural differences.

2. I should look up information about the country on the Internet.

   _____

3. Business people should learn about the customs of other countries.

   _____

(continued)

173

4. The visitor should bring a gift.

_____

5. We should be careful.

_____

3 | AFFIRMATIVE STATEMENTS WITH *SHOULD*

*Rewrite the sentences. Use **should**.*

1. We ought to ask if it's okay.

   We should ask if it's okay.

2. I ought to learn how to speak the language.

   _____

3. Ms. Jones ought to put her e-mail address on her business card.

   _____

4. You ought to plan your trip carefully.

   _____

5. The students ought to ask more questions.

   _____

4 | AFFIRMATIVE AND NEGATIVE STATEMENTS WITH *SHOULD*

*Complete the sentences. Use **should** or **shouldn't** and the words in the box.*

go to the dentist	look for another one	study more	wash it
leave a tip	~~see a doctor~~	touch it	watch it
leave early	smoke		

1. Dave is sick. He _should see a doctor._

2. I don't like my job. I _____

3. John often has a bad cough. He _____

4. Myra has a toothache. She _____

5. The car is dirty. We _____

6. The waiter is terrible. We _____

7. Doug and Jason aren't doing well in math. They _____

8. There's going to be a lot of traffic. We _____

9. That movie is very violent. The children _____

10. That dog may bite. You _____

5 | WH- QUESTIONS WITH SHOULD

Complete the conversation. Write questions with **should.** *Use* **who, what, when, where, why,** *or* **how many** *and the verbs in parentheses.*

A: Let's have a party.

B: Okay. _____ *When should we have* _____ it?
                                      1. (have)

A: Let's have it on March 23rd.

B: _____ it then?
                          2. (have)

A: Because it's Lucy's birthday.

B: Oh, that's right. _____?
                                  3. (invite)

A: Probably around 25 people.

B: _____?
                          4. (invite)

A: Let's see . . . the neighbors, Lucy's family, the people from the office.

B: _____?
                          5. (buy)

A: Well, we'll need drinks, potato chips, and things like that.

B: _____?
                          6. (cook)

A: I'll make some lasagna.

B: That sounds good. I'll make some salad. _____ a birthday cake?
                                            7. (get)

A: I like the Savoy Bakery's cakes.

B: Okay. Let's order one from there.

A: You know, we don't have enough dishes and glasses for 25 people.

_____?
                8. (do)

B: That's no problem. We can get paper plates and cups at the supermarket.

A: You're right. That's a good idea. _____ out the invitations?
                                    9. (send)

B: I'll write them this weekend.

6 | AFFIRMATIVE AND NEGATIVE STATEMENTS WITH *HAD BETTER*

Match the situations with the advice.

__c__ **1.** We'd better take a taxi.   **a.** We're lost.

____ **2.** We'd better ask for directions.   **b.** We're getting red.

____ **3.** We'd better not stay up late.   **c.** We're going to be late.

____ **4.** We'd better make sure everything is locked. **d.** We'll be away for three weeks.

____ **5.** We'd better look at a map.   **e.** We have an exam tomorrow.

____ **6.** We'd better not wait for the bus.

____ **7.** We'd better not stay in the sun anymore.

____ **8.** We'd better get a good night's sleep.

____ **9.** We'd better throw away the food in the refrigerator.

____ **10.** We'd better put some sunblock on our arms and legs.

7 | AFFIRMATIVE AND NEGATIVE STATEMENTS WITH *HAD BETTER*

*Don and Amy are planning a dinner party. Complete the conversation. Use **had better** or* **had better not** *and the words in the box.*

ask Costas to bring her	invite him	~~serve roast beef~~
borrow some from the neighbors	let the dog in the house	serve shrimp
get a couple of bottles	rent a video	sit together at the table

DON: What kind of food should we serve? How about roast beef?

AMY: Alan can't eat beef.

DON: Well, then we ____*had better not serve roast beef*____. How about shrimp?
                                                         1.

AMY: Joan doesn't like fish or seafood.

DON: Then we _____. How about chicken?
                                  2.

AMY: Good idea. Do we have enough drinks?

DON: Ed drinks only Diet Coke. We _____. Is Chris
                                                      3.

coming? She's allergic to animals. We _____.
                                                      4.

AMY: How is Sandy getting here? She doesn't drive and lives far from here.

DON: We _____.

                                 5.

AMY: What do you think of the seating plan?

DON: Marsha and Sophia _____. They don't like

                                 6.

each other.

AMY: I just remembered Tonya has a new boyfriend. We

_____. And Ted and Marsha are bringing

                                 7.

their children.

DON: They will probably get bored. We _____.

                                 8.

AMY: How many guests are coming? We won't have enough chairs.

DON: We _____.

                                 9.

39 Necessity: *Have to, Don't Have to, Must, Mustn't*

1 | PRESENT AND PAST AFFIRMATIVE AND NEGATIVE STATEMENTS WITH *HAVE TO*

Put a check (✓) next to the sentences that are true.

_____ 1. People in my country have to pay taxes.

_____ 2. People in my country don't have to vote.

_____ 3. Drivers in my country have to have driver's licenses.

_____ 4. Students in my country don't have to wear uniforms in high school.

_____ 5. Young people in my country don't have to do military service.

_____ 6. Women in my country had to obey their husbands 50 years ago.

_____ 7. Children in my country did not have to go to school 50 years ago.

_____ 8. Children in my country had to go to work at a young age 50 years ago.

2 | AFFIRMATIVE AND NEGATIVE STATEMENTS WITH *HAVE TO*

Complete the sentences. Use **have to** *and* **don't have to** *in each sentence.*

1. Students _____*don't have to*_____ stay in school 12 hours a day, but they

   _____*have to*_____ study.

2. Teachers _____ correct papers, but they

   _____ wear uniforms.

3. Police officers _____ speak a foreign language, but they

   _____ wear uniforms.

4. Doctors _____ study for many years, but they

   _____ know how to type.

5. Secretaries _____ work at night, but they

   _____ know how to type.

178

6. Firefighters _____ work at night, but they

_____ study for many years.

7. Fashion models _____ work seven days a week, but they

_____ worry about their appearance.

8. Farmers _____ get up early in the morning, but they

_____ worry about their appearance.

9. Basketball players _____ practice regularly, but they

_____ play a game every day.

10. Accountants _____ be good writers, but they

_____ be good with numbers.

3 | **AFFIRMATIVE AND NEGATIVE STATEMENTS WITH *HAVE TO***

Complete the conversations. Use **have to**, **has to**, **don't have to**, *or* **doesn't have to**.

1. **A:** Is Dan getting up early this morning?

   B: No, he _____ *doesn't have to get up early this morning* _____. There's no school.

2. **A:** Is Sheila leaving early today?

   B: Yes, she _____. She has an appointment with her dentist.

3. **A:** Are you going food shopping today?

   B: Yes, I _____. There's no food in the house.

4. **A:** Are you and your wife taking a taxi?

   B: Yes, we _____. Our car isn't working.

5. **A:** Is Barbara working late today?

   B: No, she _____. Her boss is on vacation.

6. **A:** Are the children cleaning up their room?

   B: No, they _____. I cleaned it up yesterday.

7. **A:** Is Mary taking some medicine?

   B: Yes, she _____. She has a stomach problem.

8. **A:** Are you paying for the tickets?

   B: No, we _____. They're free.

(continued)

9. **A:** Is José, wearing a suit and tie this morning?

   B: Yes, he _____. He has an important business meeting.

10. **A:** Does Bonnie do housework?

   B: No, she _____. She has a maid.

4 | PRESENT AND PAST AFFIRMATIVE AND NEGATIVE STATEMENTS WITH *HAVE TO*

Rewrite the sentences. Use **have to, has to, don't have to, doesn't have to, had to,** *or* **didn't have to**.

1. It's necessary for me to finish this exercise.

   I have to finish this exercise.

2. It isn't necessary for me to write everything 10 times.

   _____

3. It wasn't necessary for the teacher to come early yesterday.

   _____

4. It was necessary for one student to stay after class yesterday.

   _____

5. It isn't necessary for me to check e-mail every day.

   _____

6. It wasn't necessary for my friends to work last week.

   _____

7. It's necessary for the school to have clean classrooms.

   _____

8. It isn't necessary for the teacher to work on the weekend.

   _____

9. It's necessary for my classmates and me to pay attention in class.

   _____

10. It's necessary for me to write down the new words.

   _____

5 | AFFIRMATIVE AND NEGATIVE STATEMENTS WITH *MUST*

What does each sign mean? Write sentences. Use **must** *or* **mustn't** *and the words in the box.*

drive faster than 55 mph	make a U-turn	stop
~~enter~~	park in this area	turn left
go more slowly	pass	turn right

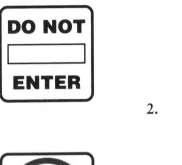

1.

2.

3.

4.

5.

6.

7.

8.

9.

1. _You mustn't enter._

2. _____

3. _____

4. _____

5. _____

6. _____

7. _____

8. _____

9. _____

6 | AFFIRMATIVE AND NEGATIVE STATEMENTS WITH *HAD TO*

Mr. and Mrs. Chung were on vacation last week. Write sentences. Use **had to** *or* **didn't have to**.

~~do any work~~	look for a hotel
find someone to take care of their dog	make the bed every morning
get to the airport on time	pack and unpack suitcases
get up early every morning	pay their hotel bill
go to work	wash dishes

1. *They didn't have to do any work.*

2. _____

3. _____

4. _____

5. _____

6. _____

7. _____

8. _____

9. _____

10. _____

7 | PAST AND PRESENT *YES / NO* QUESTIONS AND SHORT ANSWERS WITH *HAVE TO*

Write questions. Use **have to**. *Then answer the questions. Use short answers.*

1. have / English / in class / you / to / Do / speak

    Do you have to speak English in class?

    Yes, we do. (OR *No, we don't.*)

2. get up / to / your / have / Does / in the morning / at six o'clock / mother

    _____

    _____

3. you / to / last night / cook / Did / have

    _____

    _____

4. best friend / do / Does / to / have / your / this exercise

_____

_____

5. to / you / on time / in / have / English class / Do / be

_____

_____

6. friends / learn / to / Do / English / your / have

_____

_____

7. shave / father / have / your / Did / to / yesterday

_____

_____

8. your / to work / to / best friend / yesterday / Did / have / go

_____

_____

9. a / to / test / you / have / Did / last week / take

_____

_____

8 | PAST AND PRESENT *WH-* QUESTIONS WITH *HAVE TO*

Write questions. Use **have to**.

1. I have to see someone.

Who _do you have to see?_ _____

2. She has to take a test.

When _____

3. He has to leave early.

Why _____

4. The students had to wait for their teacher.

How long _____

(continued)

5. We had to meet after class.

   Why _____

6. The teacher has to talk to the parents of some students.

   How many parents _____

7. He had to pay a lot for the class.

   How much _____

8. She has to buy a lot of books.

   How many books _____

9. I have to finish my paper.

   When _____

10. The schools had to close.

    What time _____

The Comparative

1 | COMPARATIVE FORM OF ADJECTIVES

Put a check (✔) next to the statements that are true.

__✓__ 1. Elephants are bigger than cows.

_____ 2. Los Angeles is farther from New York than Chicago is.

_____ 3. Libraries are noisier than nightclubs.

_____ 4. Cell phones are more expensive than computers.

_____ 5. Trains are faster than planes.

_____ 6. Adults are younger than children.

_____ 7. Driving is more dangerous than walking.

2 | COMPARATIVE FORM OF ADJECTIVES

Put the words in the box in the correct columns.

~~big~~	dangerous	fast	hot	noisy
~~careful~~	difficult	friendly	intelligent	old
~~comfortable~~	easy	heavy	long	pretty
crowded	expensive	high	messy	small

ONE SYLLABLE	TWO SYLLABLES	THREE OR FOUR SYLLABLES
big	*careful*	*comfortable*

3 | COMPARATIVE FORM OF ADJECTIVES

Complete the sentences. Use the comparative form of the adjectives.

1. That car is old, but this car is _____older_____.

2. That book is good, but this book is _____.

3. The train station is far, but the airport is _____.

4. Tom is intelligent, but his brother is _____.

5. The service at that restaurant is bad, but the food is _____.

6. My sister's messy, but my brother is _____.

7. This chair is comfortable, but that chair is _____.

8. My husband is careful, but his father is _____.

9. This picture is pretty, but that picture is _____.

10. Chemistry is difficult, but physics is _____.

11. This exercise is easy, but the last exercise was _____.

4 | COMPARATIVE FORM OF ADJECTIVES

Complete the sentences with the correct adjectives. Use the comparative form of the adjectives in parentheses and **than**.

1. San Francisco is _____smaller than_____ New York.
   (big / small)

2. The Nile River is _____ the Mississippi River.
   (long / short)

3. A Mercedes is _____ a Volkswagen.
   (cheap / expensive)

4. An ocean is _____ a lake.
   (big / small)

5. Mountains are _____ hills.
   (low / high)

6. Egypt is _____ Canada.
   (cold / hot)

7. Skiing is _____ golf.
   (safe / dangerous)

8. Cities are _____ villages.
   (crowded / empty)

9. Cars are _____ bicycles.
   (noisy / quiet)

10. A rock is _____ a leaf.
    (heavy / light)

11. Rabbits are _____ snails.
    (slow / fast)

12. Dogs are _____ wolves.
    (friendly / unfriendly)

5 | COMPARATIVE FORM OF ADJECTIVES

Write questions. Use the comparative form of the adjectives. Then answer the questions.

1. your mother / old / or / young / your father

   Is your mother older or younger than your father?   *She is younger. (OR She's older.)*

2. which / difficult / English / your language

   Which is more difficult, English or your language?   *English.*

3. this book / cheap / or / expensive / your notebook

   _____   _____

4. your country / big / or / small / Canada

   _____   _____

5. your English pronunciation / good / or / bad / last year

   _____   _____

6. which / interesting / romantic movies / war movies

   _____   _____

7. which / healthy / coffee / tea

   _____   _____

8. which / nice / dinner at home / dinner in a restaurant

   _____   _____

1 | ADJECTIVES VS. ADVERBS

*Write **adjective** if the underlined word is an adjective. Write **adverb** if it is an adverb.*

1. I work <u>hard</u>. _____adverb_____

2. The car is <u>dirty</u>. _____adjective_____

3. Cab drivers should drive <u>carefully</u>. _____

4. This exercise isn't <u>hard</u>. _____

5. My husband always gets up <u>early</u>. _____

6. I don't want to do <u>badly</u> on the test. _____

7. That girl runs <u>fast</u>. _____

8. That jacket looks <u>good</u> on you. _____

9. Those shoes are <u>ugly</u>. _____

10. I want to speak English <u>fluently</u>. _____

11. Talk <u>slowly</u>. _____

12. I am <u>hungry</u>. _____

2 | ADVERBS OF MANNER

Circle the 10 adverbs in the box.

B	H	A	P	P	I	L	Y	F	A	X	M
A	E	A	S	I	L	Y	Q	A	X	D	O
D	A	N	G	E	R	O	U	S	L	Y	S
L	V	G	X	X	C	X	I	T	E	X	X
Y	I	R	P	A	T	I	E	N	T	L	Y
X	L	I	A	F	X	X	T	O	C	X	D
E	Y	L	S	W	E	L	L	B	N	O	R
X	X	Y	N	X	N	L	Y	I	K	X	E

3 | ADVERBS OF MANNER

Complete the sentences. Use the adverbs in Exercise 2.

1. It's snowing _____heavily_____. We can't drive in this weather.

2. Please talk _____. The baby's sleeping.

3. Vinny drives _____. One day he's going to have an accident.

4. Lenore was an hour late for class. Her teacher looked at her _____.

5. The children played with their toys _____.

6. She plays the guitar very _____. Everyone loves to listen to her.

7. I never eat my father's food. He cooks _____.

8. I can't understand him. He speaks _____.

9. I waited _____. but the doctor never came.

10. Your directions were very good. I found the restaurant _____.

4 | ADJECTIVES AND ADVERBS

Complete the conversations. Use the adjectives in the box or their adverb forms.

angry	careful	fast	~~quiet~~	tired
bad	easy	good	serious	

1. A: Shh! Be _____quiet_____! This is a library.

   B: Talk _____quietly_____.

2. A: The potatoes taste _____.

   B: Yes, they are very _____. I'll have some more.

3. A: Is Nicole a _____ runner?

   B: Yes, she runs very _____. She wins races all the time.

4. A: Go to bed. You look _____.

   B: But I'm not _____.

5. A: Is Martha _____ with her boyfriend?

   B: I think so. Yesterday she spoke to him _____, and now she's not talking

   to him.

(continued)

6. **A:** Is Kim a _____ typist?

   B: Yes, she types _____. She never makes mistakes.

7. **A:** Were the directions _____?

   B: Yes, I made the cake _____. I didn't have any problems at all.

8. **A:** Why are you so unhappy? Was the game _____?

   B: Yes, it was. We lost. Everybody played _____.

9. **A:** Kevin's always so _____. He hardly ever smiles.

   B: I know. He does everything so _____.

Enough; Too / Very; As + Adjective + As; Same / Different

1 | TOO AND ENOUGH

Match the questions and answers.

_c_	1. Do you want to go to the movies with us?	a. No, it's too cold.
____	2. Can I go to the party tonight?	b. No, it's too expensive.
____	3. Why are you looking for a new apartment?	c. No, it's too late.
____	4. Are you going to the beach today?	d. No, he's too fussy.
____	5. Are you going to buy the necklace?	e. He's not serious enough.
____	6. Is your son on the swim team?	f. No, he's not fast enough.
____	7. Why doesn't Joe do well in school?	g. Ours isn't big enough.
____	8. Do you like to cook for Adam?	h. No, you're not old enough.

2 | TOO + ADJECTIVE

*Rewrite the sentences. Use **too**.*

1. The box isn't light enough to carry.

   The box is too heavy to carry.
   _____

2. The questions aren't easy enough to answer.

   _____

3. The shirt isn't big enough to wear.

   _____

4. It isn't cool enough outside to go running.

   _____

(continued)

191

5. The store isn't close enough to walk.

_____

6. The soup isn't hot enough to eat.

_____

3 | ADJECTIVE + *NOT ENOUGH*

*Rewrite the sentences. Use **not enough**.*

1. It's too noisy in here to talk.

   It's not quiet enough in here to talk.

2. The story was too boring.

   _____

3. Your room is too messy.

   _____

4. Your hair is too long.

   _____

5. You're too young to watch that kind of TV program.

   _____

6. The numbers are too small to see.

   _____

4 | *TOO* AND *VERY*

*Complete the sentences. Use **too** or **very**.*

1. **A:** Do you like my new shirt?

   B: Yes, it's _____*very*_____ nice.

2. **A:** Put these sweaters in the drawer.

   B: I can't. The drawer's _____ full.

3. **A:** Mommy, I want to swim in the baby pool.

   B: You're _____ big. You're not a baby.

4. **A:** What do you think of that hotel?

   B: The rooms are _____ nice, but it's expensive.

5. **A:** How's the weather in Montreal in January?

   B: It's _____ cold.

6. **A:** Can you read that sign?

   B: No, it's _____ far away.

7. **A:** Are you going to buy the stereo?

   B: I think so. The price is _____ good.

8. **A:** The floor's _____ dirty.

   B: I'll wash it.

9. **A:** Put this bag in your pocket.

   B: I can't. It's _____ big.

5 | *TOO* OR *ENOUGH* + INFINITIVE

*Combine the sentences. Use **too** or **enough** and an infinitive.*

1. You can't marry him. He's too old.

   He's too old to marry.

2. You can't buy that cell phone. It's too expensive.

   _____

3. I can't wait. I'm too tired.

   _____

4. Sandra didn't eat the steak. It was too tough.

   _____

5. Jeffrey can't drive. He isn't old enough.

   _____

6. They can't play on the team. They aren't good enough.

   _____

7. I can't drink the tea. It's too hot.

   _____

8. She can do the work. She's smart enough.

   _____

6 | TOO, ENOUGH, AND NOT ENOUGH

*Complete the conversations. Use **too**, **enough**, or **not enough** and the adjective in parentheses.*

1. **A:** Why did you take the pants back to the store?

   B: They were _____ too long _____. I exchanged them for a shorter pair.
   (long)

2. **A:** Do you want me to wash the car again?

   B: Yes. It's _____ not clean enough _____.
   (clean)

3. **A:** Let's go into that big old house. I want to see what's in there.

   B: No, I'm _____. There may be ghosts.
   (frightened)

4. **A:** Are the shoes comfortable?

   B: No, they're _____. I need a size 8, and they're a size 7.
   (big)

5. **A:** Why didn't you get the tickets?

   B: It was _____. There weren't any left.
   (late)

6. **A:** Is the soup _____?
   (hot)

   B: Yeah. Thanks for heating it up.

7. **A:** How are the pants?

   B: They're _____. I think I need a larger size.
   (tight)

8. **A:** Why do I need to rewrite this composition?

   B: Because it's _____. It's only 150 words, and I told you to write at
   (short)
   least 250 words.

9. **A:** Can I borrow your bike?

   B: No, there's something wrong with the brakes. It's _____ to ride.
   (safe)

10. **A:** Dad, can we go in the water now?

    B: I don't know. It was cold before. Put your toe in the water and see if it's

    _____ now.
    (warm)

11. **A:** Why aren't the plants in the living room growing?

    B: Probably because it's _____. They need more light.
    (sunny)

7 | AS + ADJECTIVE + AS, *THE SAME* (+ NOUN) *AS, DIFFERENT FROM*

Put a check (✓) next to the statements that are true.

_____ 1. Canada is the same size as the United States.

_____ 2. Lions are not as big as elephants.

_____ 3. 32°F is the same temperature as 0°C.

_____ 4. The Statue of Liberty in New York is not as old as the Pyramids in Egypt.

_____ 5. Alaska is as cold as Antarctica.

_____ 6. A whale is different from a fish.

_____ 7. An orange is the same color as a carrot.

_____ 8. Silver is as valuable as gold.

8 | *THAN* AND *AS*

Complete the sentences. Use **as** *or* **than**.

1. Russia is bigger ___than___ the United States.

2. Is your classroom the same size ___as___ the other classrooms?

3. South America is not as big _____ Asia.

4. English is more difficult _____ my native language.

5. The president of the United States is not the same age _____ the leader of my country.

6. I'm more tired today _____ I was yesterday.

7. Are doctors as rich _____ lawyers?

8. Are you as thin _____ your best friend?

9. Thelma's the same height _____ her brother.

10. Are animals more intelligent _____ human beings?

11. This book is better _____ that one.

12. Some people are friendlier _____ others.

9 | AS + ADJECTIVE + AS AND MORE + ADJECTIVE + THAN

Write sentences. Use the adjective in parentheses and **as . . . as**, **not as . . . as,** *or* **more . . . than**. *(Remember: = means* **equals**, *< means* **less than**, *> means* **more than**.*)*

1. a Hyundai < a Mercedes (expensive)

   A Hyundai isn't as expensive as a Mercedes.

2. the book > the film (interesting)

   The book is more interesting than the film.

3. my apartment = your apartment (big)

   My apartment is as big as your apartment.

4. trains < airplanes (fast)

   _____

5. January = February (cold)

   _____

6. the chair = the sofa (comfortable)

   _____

7. the governor of Oregon < the president of the United States (famous)

   _____

8. the bank < the post office (far)

   _____

9. limes = lemons (sour)

   _____

10. jazz > rock music (relaxing)

    _____

11. chocolate ice cream < vanilla ice cream (good)

    _____

12. some people > other people (violent)

    _____

13. college < high school (easy)

    _____

14. these boxes = those boxes (heavy)

    _____

10 | THE SAME + NOUN + AS

Write questions. Use **the same . . . as** and a noun in the box.

age	~~color~~	distance	height	length	price	size	weight

1. *Is your sister's hair the same color as your hair?*

   No. My sister's hair is brown. My hair's black.

2. _____

   No. I'm 1.69 meters tall. My brother's 1.78 meters tall.

3. _____

   No. My mother's 59 years old. My father's 62.

4. _____

   No. The dining room's smaller than the living room.

5. _____

   Yes. The apples and the oranges are both 60¢ a pound.

6. _____

   No. I'm thinner than my brother.

7. _____

   No. *War and Peace* is much longer than *Crime and Punishment*.

8. _____

   No. The subway station is farther than the bus stop.

11 | THE SAME AS AND DIFFERENT FROM

Write sentences. Use **the same as** or **different from**.

1. a wife and a housewife

   A wife is different from a housewife.

2. the U.S.A. and the United States

   The U.S.A. is the same as the United States.

3. a bike and a bicycle

   _____

(continued)

4. a TV and a television

_____

5. North America and the United States

_____

6. 10,362 and 10.362

_____

7. 3×16 and 16×3

_____

8. $16 \div 3$ and $3 \div 16$

_____

9. $1 and £1

_____

10. a snack bar and a restaurant

_____

11. 12:00 P.M. and noon

_____

12. a plane and an airplane

_____

The Superlative

1 | THE SUPERLATIVE FORM OF ADJECTIVES

Look at the restaurant reviews and answer the questions.

Donnelly's	The Big Oven	Circo	Shanghai Garden	
$$$$	$$	$$$	$	Prices
7.5	9.5	7	10	Quality of Food
7.5	10	8	7.5	Friendly Staff
10	9	7	9.5	Cleanliness
9	9.5	10	7	Atmosphere
35 tables	20 tables	60 tables	35 tables	Size
8.5	**9.5**	**8**	**8.5**	**Overall Rating**

Which restaurant . . . ?

1. is the most expensive?   _____Donnelly's_____

2. has the most delicious food?   _____

3. has the friendliest staff?   _____

4. is the cleanest?   _____

5. is the biggest?   _____

6. has the nicest atmosphere?   _____

7. is the best?   _____

2 | THE SUPERLATIVE FORM OF ADJECTIVES

Complete the sentences. Use the superlative form of the adjective.

1. The kitchen is always hot. It's _____ *the hottest* _____ room in the house.

2. Roger's a bad student. He's _____ student in the class.

3. Chemistry is hard. For me, it's _____ subject in school.

4. Roses are beautiful. I think that roses are _____ flowers.

5. Noon is a busy time at the bank. In fact, it's _____ time.

6. *Married Young* is a funny program. It's _____ program on TV.

7. Scully's is a good restaurant. In fact, it's _____ restaurant in town.

8. Monkeys are ugly. In my opinion, they're _____ animals in the zoo.

9. Midnight is a popular nightclub. It's _____ nightclub in town.

10. Dixon's has low prices. It has _____ prices in the neighborhood.

11. Pamela's a fast swimmer. She's _____ swimmer on the team.

12. Jake is charming. He's _____ of all my friends.

3 | THE SUPERLATIVE AND *ONE OF THE*

*Write questions with **one of the** and the superlative adjective. Then answer the questions.*

1. What / long / rivers in the world?

   _____ *What is one of the longest rivers in the world?* _____ _____ *The Mississippi.* _____

2. What / tall / buildings in the world?

   _____ _____

3. What / crowded / cities in the world?

   _____ _____

4. What / famous / buildings in the world?

   _____ _____

5. What / polluted / places in the world?

   _____ _____

6. Who / good / athletes in the world?

   _____ _____

4 | THE COMPARATIVE AND SUPERLATIVE FORM OF ADJECTIVES

Write two sentences. Use the superlative form of the adjective in parentheses for one sentence. Use the comparative form for the other.

1. a train / a plane / a bus (fast)

   a. *A plane is the fastest of the three.*

   b. *A train is faster than a bus.*

2. a teenager / a child / a baby (old)

   a. _____

   b. _____

3. Nigeria / Spain / Sweden (hot)

   a. _____

   b. _____

4. a street / a path / a highway (wide)

   a. _____

   b. _____

5. a city / a village / a town (big)

   a. _____

   b. _____

6. an elephant / a gorilla / a fox (heavy)

   a. _____

   b. _____

7. an hour / a second / a minute (long)

   a. _____

   b. _____

8. boxing / golf / soccer (dangerous)

   a. _____

   b. _____

Workbook Answer Key

In this answer key, where the contracted form is given, the full form is often also correct, and where the full form is given, the contracted form is often also correct.

UNIT 1 (pages 1–5)

1

2. is
3. am
4. is
5. are
6. is
7. are
8. is
9. is
10. am

2

2. we
3. She
4. It
5. He
6. It
7. They
8. We
9. They
10. He
11. He
12. It

3

Sentences with: I am / My best friend is / My mother is / My father is / My teacher is / My parents are / My classmates are

4

2. California is not a country. It is a state.
3. Russia is not small. It is big.
4. Egypt and China are not people. They are countries.
5. Boston and New York are not in Canada. They are in the United States.
6. Florida is not a city. It is a state.
7. The sun is not cold. It is hot.
8. Toyotas and Fords are not airplanes. They are cars.
9. Ottawa is not the capital of the United States. Washington, D.C., is the capital of the United States. (OR Ottawa is the capital of Canada.)
10. Cigarettes are not good for people. They are bad for people.
11. The sun and the moon are not near Earth. They are far from Earth.

5

2. is
3. is not
4. are not
5. are
6. are not
7. is
8. is not
9. are
10. is not

6

2. We are from New York. I am from New York, too.
3. I am a big baseball fan. I am not.
4. Jessica is a very good soccer player. She is a good student, too.
5. You are Mark, right? No, I am not Mark. I am his brother Mike.
6. Pedro is 19. No, he is not. He is 16.
7. Volleyball is a popular sport. Soccer is popular, too. They are not popular in my country.

7

2. Yung-Hee and Ali aren't in class today. They're at a game.
3. The teacher's not in class. I know. She's sick.
4. Antonio's a student in your class. His name's not on my list.
5. Melinda's a good singer. She's pretty, too.
6. I'm right. No, you're not. You're wrong.
7. They're my books. No, they're not. They're my books.

8

My favorite sport **is** baseball. It **is** popular in the United States. My favorite players are Pedro Martínez and Orlando Cabrera. **They** are baseball players in the United States. But they **are** not from the United States. Pedro **Martínez is** from the Dominican Republic. Orlando Cabrera is **not** from the Dominican Republic. He's from Colombia.

UNIT 2 (pages 6–8)

1

3. Are you hungry?
4. Are you and your classmates unhappy?
5. Is your teacher in school today?
6. We are very good students.
7. I am very thirsty.
8. Is your watch expensive?
9. Michigan is near Canada.
10. Are the students from the same country?
11. Is your car comfortable?
12. This exercise is easy.

2

2. f	**5.** l	**8.** k	**11.** a
3. h	**6.** c	**9.** i	**12.** b
4. j	**7.** g	**10.** e	

3

Some answers will vary.

2. Are you happy? Yes, I am. (OR No, I'm not.)

3. Is your mother a student? Yes, she is. (OR No, she isn't.)

4. Is today Thursday? Yes, it is. (OR No, it isn't.)

5. Are your friends from California? No, they're not. (OR No, they aren't.)

6. Is your friend busy? No, she isn't.

7. Are you a singer? No, I'm not.

8. Is your teacher friendly? Yes, she / he is. (OR No, she / he isn't.)

9. Are your mother and father Canadian? No, they aren't. (OR No, they're not.)

10. Are you married? Yes, I am. (OR No, I'm not.)

11. Are your classmates young? No, they're not. (OR No, they aren't).

12. Is it 11 o'clock? Yes, it is. (OR No, it isn't.)

4

Yes, it **is**.

Oh. **Are we** late for class?

Yes, you are.

Are you Ana Leite and Fernando Romeiro from Brazil?

No, **we're not.**

No, I don't think **so**.

UNIT 3 (pages 9–11)

1

Answers will vary.

2

3. William Shakespeare and Charles Dickens weren't Canadian.

4. Bill Clinton wasn't the first president of the United States.

5. Charlie Chaplin and Marilyn Monroe were movie stars.

6. The end of World War I wasn't in 1942.

7. *Titanic* was the name of a movie.

8. Toronto and Washington, D.C., weren't big cities 300 years ago.

9. Indira Gandhi and Napoleon were famous people.

10. Nelson Mandela was a political leader.

11. Oregon and Hawaii weren't part of the United States in 1776.

12. Disneyland wasn't a famous place 100 years ago.

3

Answers will vary.

2. Were you a student 10 years ago? Yes, I was. (OR No, I wasn't.)

3. Were you in English class yesterday? Yes, I was. (OR No, I wasn't.)

4. Were all the students in class last week? Yes, they were. (OR No, they weren't.)

5. Was the weather nice yesterday? Yes, it was. (OR No, it wasn't.)

6. Was your teacher at work two days ago. Yes, she / he was. (OR No, she / he wasn't.)

4

3. is	**9.** is	**15.** were
4. is	**10.** was	**16.** was
5. is	**11.** was	**17.** were
6. are	**12.** were	**18.** were
7. is	**13.** Were	**19.** Are
8. Is	**14.** were	**20.** are

UNIT 4 (pages 12–14)

1

2. a	**4.** h	**6.** c	**8.** g
3. e	**5.** f	**7.** b	

2

2. Tom Cruise is an actor.

3. Elizabeth II is a queen.

4. Céline Dion is a singer.

5. Neil Armstrong is an astronaut.

6. Yo Yo Ma is a musician.

7. Hillary Clinton is a politician.

8. J. K. Rowling is an author.

3

/z/—dictionaries, girls, lemons, sons

/ɪz/—boxes, classes, houses, watches

/s/—roommates, states, students, notebooks

4

3. men	**7.** continents	**11.** universities
4. songs	**8.** states	**12.** watches
5. cities	**9.** countries	**13.** actors
6. rivers	**10.** provinces	**14.** mountains

5

2. 2 children, 3 children

3. 6 teeth, 7 teeth

4. 1 foot, 4 feet

5. 1 grandchild, 7 grandchildren

6. 1 person, 9 people

7. 2 sisters-in-law, 3 sisters-in-law

6

3. They're clothes.
4. They're photos.
5. It's an umbrella.
6. It's an eraser.
7. They're lips.
8. It's a bird.
9. They're teeth.
10. It's a hat.
11. They're pants.
12. It's an earring.

UNIT 5 (pages 15–17)

1

2. difficult
3. boring
4. unfriendly
5. new
6. small
7. uncomfortable
8. ugly
9. old
10. warm

2

2. They are honest men.
3. They are tall girls.
4. They are intelligent animals.
5. Those books are expensive.
6. Eggs are white or brown.
7. They are good actors.
8. These watches are cheap.
9. They are interesting stories.

3

2. It is a long movie.
3. The Prado is a famous museum.
4. You are an unusual photographer.
5. They are interesting buildings.
6. He is an intelligent man.
7. It is a crowded village.
8. She is a popular soccer player.
9. We are good students.
10. This is an easy exercise.

UNIT 6 (pages 18–20)

1

Answers will vary.

2

2. between
3. next to (OR near)
4. near
5. in
6. near
7. between
8. in
9. next to
10. near

3

2. in
3. In
4. in
5. On
6. on
7. At
8. on
9. on
10. in

UNIT 7 (pages 21–23)

1

3. Who
4. Why
5. Where
6. What
7. Why
8. Where
9. Who
10. What
11. Where
12. What

2

3. What sports are you good at? Soccer and basketball.
4. Where are they from? Brazil.
5. Who was the woman in your garden? My best friend.
6. Why is your mother in bed? Because she's tired.
7. Where are my shoes? Under the bed.
8. What was in the bag? A sandwich.
9. Where is (OR Where's) the post office? On Park Street.
10. Who is (OR Who's) your favorite writer? Shakespeare.
11. Why is the class popular? Because it's interesting.
12. What is (OR What's) in the tree? A bird.

3

2. Why
3. Where
4. Why
5. What
6. Who
7. Where

4

2. Where's the hospital?
3. Who was John Wayne?
4. Where's Room 203?
5. Where are my keys?
6. Who were Nelson Mandela and Boris Yeltsin?
7. Who was (that) on the phone?
8. What are Cadillacs?
9. What's that (OR this)?
10. Where's the wastepaper basket?
11. Where were you last night?

UNIT 8 (pages 24–27)

1

2. They're secretaries.
3. He's a pilot.
4. She's a professor.
5. They're flight attendants.
6. You're a cook.
7. You're a salesperson.
8. She's a doctor.

2

2. teaches	5. plays	8. paint
3. sings	6. manages	9. washes
4. dances	7. collect	10. fight

3

2. take	10. lives	18. doesn't come
3. goes	11. has	19. isn't
4. has	12. is	20. helps
5. live	13. doesn't have	21. go
6. don't live	14. live	22. don't have
7. have	15. studies	23. try
8. don't live	16. works	24. don't get
9. is	17. leaves	

4

2. Water doesn't boil at 90°C. It boils at 100°C.
3. Water doesn't freeze at 5°C. It freezes at 0°C.
4. The sun doesn't go around the Earth. The Earth goes around the sun.
5. Penguins don't come from the Arctic. They come from the Antarctic.
6. Cows don't eat meat. They eat grass.
7. China doesn't have a small population. It has a big population.
8. Deserts don't have a lot of water. They have a lot of sand.
9. Elephants don't have small ears. They have big ears.
10. Egypt doesn't have a cold climate. It has a hot climate.
11. The sun doesn't shine at night. It shines during the day.
12. Cats don't run after dogs. Dogs run after cats.

UNIT 9 (pages 28–31)

1

2. A	5. C	8. A	11. D
3. D	6. B	9. C	12. C
4. A	7. D	10. B	

2

2. f	4. a	6. g	8. d
3. c	5. b	7. h	

3

3. Yes, she does.	7. No, they don't.
4. No, she doesn't.	8. No, he doesn't.
5. Yes, they do.	9. Yes, they do.
6. Yes, she does.	10. No, they don't.

4

3. doesn't	6. don't	9. don't
4. doesn't	7. don't	10. doesn't
5. don't	8. don't	

5

2. Does your roommate like your girlfriend?
3. Does the teacher wear glasses?
4. Does Mr. Flagg have a car?
5. Do Jack and Jill sleep until 10 o'clock?
6. Does Peter eat fast?
7. Does she leave for work at the same time every day?
8. Does the dog eat two times a day?
9. Does the doctor have your telephone number?
10. Do football players play in the summer?

6

2. Does he have	8. Does she wear
3. Do they like	9. Do you like
4. Do you live	10. Do you know
5. Does he know	11. Do they work
6. Do you want	12. Does he come
7. Do you have	

UNIT 10 (pages 32–35)

1

3. Where	8. Where
4. What	9. When
5. Who	10. Why
6. When	11. How
7. Who	12. When

2

2. What do you have for breakfast? Cereal.
3. How do you feel after a nap? Great.
4. Who corrects your homework? My teacher.
5. Where does Rosita work? At City Central Bank.
6. When do you and your family go on vacation? In August.
7. What do you wear to work? A suit and tie.
8. Why do you need more money? Because I want to buy a sweatshirt.
9. What time do the kids eat lunch? At noon.
10. When does the mail come? In the morning.
11. Where does Doug play soccer? At his school.
12. Who does Mark visit on Sundays? His friends.

3

2. How	6. When
3. Why	7. Why
4. What	8. What
5. Where	

4

2. Why do you drink tea at night?
3. What do you remember about your dream?
4. How does your roommate look in the morning?
5. Why do teenagers sleep late?
6. Where does your roommate sleep?
7. Who (usually) wakes you up?
8. When do you sleep late?
9. Who sleeps in the small bedroom?
10. What do you do after your nap?
11. Who sleeps a lot in your family?
12. Who does she want to wake up?

UNIT 11 (pages 36–41)

1

At—night; half past six
In—the morning; the summer; the evening; 1888; May; the spring
On—June 30th; December 3rd; March 20, 2006; Thursday

2

2. It's at 1:30.
3. It's at 10:30.
4. It's on Sunday morning.
5. It's on Saturday.
6. It's at 2:00.
7. It's at seven o'clock.
8. No, it's in the afternoon.
9. It's at 3 P.M.

3

3. what is the date? (OR what day is it?)
4. what time is it?
5. when is it?
6. when is it?
7. what time is it? (OR when is it?)
8. when is it open?
9. when is your birthday? (OR what day is your birthday?)

4

3. 9th
4. 12th
5. 23rd
6. 51st
7. 72nd
8. 80th
9. 95th
10. 101st
11. 116th
12. 200th

5

3. third
4. eleventh
5. fifteenth
6. twentieth
7. thirty-first
8. forty-seventh
9. sixty-sixth
10. eighty-second
11. ninety-ninth
12. one hundred and third

6

2. Twenty-third Street and First Avenue
3. Forty-third Street and Tenth Avenue
4. Fifty-second Street and Sixth Avenue
5. Eighty-sixth Street and Fifth Avenue
6. Fourteenth Street and Eighth Avenue
7. Sixty-ninth Street and Second Avenue

7

2. It's on May twenty-third.
3. It's on May second.
4. It's on April first.
5. It's on May thirtieth.
6. It's on April fifteenth.
7. It's on April twenty-fifth.
8. It's on May eleventh.
9. It's on May twenty-eighth.
10. It's on April twentieth.

UNIT 12 (pages 42–48)

1

2. e
3. a
4. b
5. f
6. i
7. g
8. h
9. d

2

2. your, their
3. her, his
4. our, their
5. my, her
6. your, his, my (OR our), Her

3

2. He, His
3. She, her
4. They, Their, their, It
5. We, Our
6. I, I, My
7. She, Her
8. We, Our, Its, It, it
9. Their, They, They

4

3. Mariana's their neighbor.
4. Her last name is Martinez.
5. She's an aunt.
6. Danny and Federico are her nephews.
7. He's eight years old.
8. His eyes are blue.
9. Her dogs are always outside.
10. He's afraid of the dogs.
11. They were with their aunt yesterday.
12. She was with her dogs.
13. Their food was in the garage.
14. They were in the garage.
15. Their friends were not with them today.
16. They were happy to be with their aunt.

5

3. Whose eggs are these?
4. Whose bananas are these?
5. Whose bread is this?
6. Whose potatoes are these?
7. Whose cake is this?
8. Whose milk is this?
9. Whose orange juice is this?
10. Whose potato chips are these?
11. Whose carrots are these?
12. Whose bag is this?

6

3. Baker's
4. men's
5. husband's
6. babies'
7. girls' school
8. brothers'
9. son's
10. doctor's
11. teacher's
12. teachers'

7

2. Mrs. Simpson's
3. Mary Rose's
4. Nora's
5. Bill's
6. Joe Mott's
7. Dr. Lin's
8. Maria Lico's
9. Tom Cho's

UNIT 13 (pages 49–53)

1

2. This is a gift for you.
3. This cake is delicious. These cookies are good, too.
4. This table is expensive. These chairs are expensive, too.
5. Dana, this is Eric.
6. These earrings are only $25.
7. This is a boring party.
8. These are cool sneakers. This T-shirt is cool, too.
9. These flowers are for you.
10. These are my parents.

2

2. What's this?
3. What's this?
4. What's this?
5. What are these?
6. What are these?
7. What's this?
8. What are these?
9. What are these?
10. What's this?

3

2. that
3. those
4. those
5. Those
6. that
7. that
8. that
9. that
10. those
11. those
12. those

4

2. that
3. this
4. this
5. those
6. These
7. those
8. That
9. These
10. that

5

2. Is Vicente Mexican or Brazilian?
3. Is it December 6th or 5th?
4. Does the train arrive at 6:30 or 7:30?
5. Do you have a suitcase or a backpack?
6. Is Wayne in the east or the west?
7. Does the guide speak French or Spanish?
8. Do the people leave on Monday or Sunday?
9. Is your bag black or brown?
10. Do I need a coat or a sweater?

UNIT 14 (pages 54–55)

1

2. g
3. a
4. h
5. b
6. c
7. f
8. e

2

2. Which one do you want?
3. Do you like this one?
4. Which one is on sale?
5. Which ones does she have?
6. Which ones are for boys?
7. Is the red one from Italy, too?
8. Are the silver ones expensive, too?

3

2. No, I prefer the brown ones.
3. The one in the corner?
4. No, only the ones in the bowl.
5. This one is terrible.
6. No, but there's one about a mile away.
7. The ones on the kitchen table.
8. No, but Carla wants one.
9. I like it, too.
10. The other ones are better.
11. No, give me the ones over there.
12. But the one on Fifth Street costs less.
13. Here are your black ones.
14. It is on the table near the door.

UNIT 15 (pages 56–60)

1

2. e
3. b
4. a
5. j
6. c
7. g
8. f
9. h
10. i

2

3. smiling
4. shining
5. rain
6. make
7. sleeping
8. listening
9. run
10. holding
11. take
12. smoking
13. doing
14. put
15. begin
16. reading
17. cry
18. staying

3

3. right now
4. right now
5. these days
6. these days
7. these days
8. these days
9. right now
10. these days

4

2. aren't standing, are sitting
3. is watching, isn't reading
4. aren't reading, are reading
5. isn't running, is standing
6. is holding, isn't talking
7. is buying, isn't buying
8. are smiling, aren't crying

5

3. I am (OR am not) having a good time.
4. The sun is (OR is not) shining.
5. It is (OR is not) raining.
6. It is (OR is not) getting dark.
7. I am (OR am not) listening to the radio.
8. I am (OR am not) talking on the phone.
9. I am (OR am not) sitting on a chair.
10. My neighbors are (OR are not) making a lot of noise.

6

2. is snowing
3. are skiing
4. are relaxing
5. are sitting
6. is reading
7. am writing
8. are making
9. are enjoying
10. is playing

UNIT 16 (pages 61–68)

1

2. Are you wearing glasses? Yes, I am. (OR No, I'm not.)
3. Is your English teacher correcting papers? Yes, he / she is. (OR No, he / she isn't.)
4. Are you and a friend watching TV? Yes, we are. (OR No, we aren't.)
5. Are your classmates doing this exercise now? Yes, they are. (OR No, they aren't.)
6. Are you having dinner with your neighbors? Yes, I am. (OR No, I'm not.)

7. Is the sun shining? Yes, it is. (OR No, it isn't.)
8. Are your friends waiting for you? Yes, they are. (OR No, they aren't.)
9. Are your parents working? Yes, they are. (OR No, they aren't.)
10. Are you eating ice cream? Yes, I am. (OR No, I'm not.)
11. Is your teacher helping you? Yes, he / she is. (OR No, he / she isn't.)
12. Are children playing outside? Yes, they are. (OR No, they aren't.)

2

2. The man / her father is.
3. He's tired. *(Answers will vary)*.
4. Near the man.
5. A basketball game.
6. In a / the living room. (OR On a sofa.)
7. The little girl is.

3

2. Is she sleeping?
3. Are they playing?
4. Are they swimming?
5. Is he buying stamps?
6. Are they having a good time?
7. Is she visiting someone?
8. Are they playing tennis?
9. Is she fixing something?
10. Is he coming?
11. Are they waiting for me?
12. Is he following me?

4

2. Why are you watching a talk show?
3. What are the people talking about?
4. Who is he meeting?
5. Where are they meeting?
6. Why are they meeting at the mall?
7. Who is laughing?
8. What are they laughing about?
9. Where are you sitting?
10. What are you eating?

5

2. Who is he meeting?
3. What are you and Kevin doing?
4. What are you eating?
5. What are the people talking about?
6. Why are they meeting at the mall?
7. What are they laughing about?
8. Where are you sitting?
9. Who is laughing?
10. Where are they meeting?

6

2. a	**4.** a	**6.** b
3. b	**5.** b	**7.** a

7

2. What are you reading?
3. What are they eating?
4. What is he cooking?
5. Who's coming?
6. Why are you going to bed?
7. Where are you going?
8. Why are you selling your car?
9. Where are they swimming?
10. What are you watching?
11. Who are they watching?
12. Who is she dating?

UNIT 17 (pages 69–71)

1

2. e	**5.** a	**8.** j
3. b	**6.** i	**9.** f
4. c	**7.** g	**10.** h

2

3. Clean	**7.** Don't be	**11.** Don't use
4. Don't talk	**8.** Don't tell	**12.** Don't touch
5. Don't buy	**9.** Study	
6. Ask	**10.** Give	

3

2. Get off	**4.** turn	**6.** make
3. Go (OR Walk)	**5.** Walk (OR Go)	**7.** Ring

4

2. fill in   **3.** pick up   **4.** Send in

UNIT 18 (pages 72–74)

1

2. secretary   **3.** driver   **4.** summer camp worker

2

4. He can drive and lift 100 pounds.
5. He can type and speak Spanish.
6. She can play the guitar and draw.
7. He can't drive, and he can't lift 100 pounds.
8. She can type, but she can't speak Spanish.
9. She can lift 100 pounds, but she can't drive.
10. He can draw, but he can't play the guitar.
11. She can't draw, and she can't play the guitar.
12. He can't type, and he can't speak Spanish.

3

2. Can your mother lift 100 pounds? Yes, she can. (OR No, she can't.)
3. Can your father play the guitar? Yes, he can. (OR No, he can't.)
4. Can your best friend ride a horse? Yes, he / she can. (OR No, he / she can't.)
5. Can your parents speak Spanish? Yes, they can. (OR No, they can't.)
6. Can you swim? Yes, I can. (OR No, I can't.)
7. Can you type? Yes, I can. (OR No, I can't.)

4

2. could practice	**7.** couldn't get
3. couldn't go	**8.** could hear
4. couldn't answer	**9.** couldn't go
5. couldn't eat	**10.** could do
6. could play	

UNIT 19 (pages 75–78)

1

2. b	**5.** a	**8.** a
3. b	**6.** a	**9.** a
4. a	**7.** b	**10.** b

2

2. Let's get something to eat.
3. Let's go swimming.
4. Let's not invite her to the party.
5. Why don't we go out and look for him?
6. Why don't we go inside?
7. Why don't we leave?

3

2. e
3. b
4. a
5. d
6. (*Possible answer*) Why don't you turn on the TV?
7. (*Possible answer*) Why don't you watch movies in English?
8. (*Possible answer*) Why don't you take an aspirin?

4

2. don't, it	**5.** Okay
3. Why, instead	**6.** plan
4. Sorry, can't	**7.** Sounds

UNIT 20 (pages 79–83)

1

2. i	**4.** e	**6.** b	**8.** f
3. a	**5.** g	**7.** c	**9.** h

2

2. Last	**4.** Yesterday	**6.** yesterday
3. Last	**5.** yesterday	**7.** last

3

2. Karen learned how to drive _____ years ago.
3. Karen visited her high school friends _____ months ago.
4. Karen called her grandparents _____ days ago.
5. Karen talked to her parents _____ days ago.
6. Karen shared an apartment with friends _____ years ago.
7. Karen traveled to Hong Kong _____ months ago.
8. Karen invited some friends for dinner _____ days ago.
9. Karen worked in Miami _____ years ago.
10. Karen started her own business _____ months ago.

4

2. They played basketball
3. She washed her clothes
4. They studied
5. He worked in his garden
6. He cooked dinner at 6:00
7. She talked to her daughter
8. They traveled to France
9. It closed at 3:00 P.M.
10. They watched television

5

2. enjoyed, didn't enjoy
3. e-mailed, didn't e-mail
4. arrived, didn't arrive
5. promised, didn't promise
6. visited, didn't visit
7. tried, didn't try
8. walked, didn't walk
9. hugged, didn't hug
10. rented, didn't rent

6

2. am thinking	**10.** cleaned	**18.** danced
3. think	**11.** played	**19.** enjoyed
4. is shining	**12.** comes	**20.** am cooking
5. are singing	**13.** speak	**21.** need
6. rained	**14.** don't speak	**22.** don't want
7. stayed	**15.** laughs	**23.** know
8. didn't go	**16.** invited	
9. washed	**17.** listened	

UNIT 21 (pages 84–87)

1

3. *put*, irregular, put
4. *had*, irregular, have
5. *brushed*, regular, brush
6. *left*, irregular, leave
7. *arrived*, regular, arrive
8. *began*, irregular, begin
9. *learned*, regular, learn
10. *finished*, regular, finish
11. *met*, irregular, meet
12. *ate*, irregular, eat
13. *went*, irregular, go
14. *stayed*, regular, stay

2

2. got	**7.** said	**12.** taught
3. ate	**8.** knew	**13.** left
4. put	**9.** met	**14.** bought
5. went	**10.** came	**15.** began
6. had	**11.** sold	

3

Probable answers

2. I didn't eat 3 kilos of oranges for breakfast yesterday morning.
3. I didn't sleep 21 hours yesterday.
4. I didn't bring a horse to English class two weeks ago.
5. I didn't go to the moon last month.
6. I didn't meet the leader of my country last night.
7. I didn't find $10,000 in a brown paper bag yesterday.
8. I didn't do this exercise two years ago.
9. I didn't swim 30 kilometers yesterday.
10. I didn't speak English perfectly 10 years ago.

4

2. didn't get	**10.** ate	**18.** didn't have
3. got	**11.** took	**19.** drove
4. went	**12.** stayed	**20.** saw
5. met	**13.** looked	**21.** invited
6. went	**14.** bought	**22.** didn't eat
7. didn't see	**15.** didn't buy	**23.** watched
8. didn't have	**16.** came	**24.** didn't leave
9. closed	**17.** made	

UNIT 22 (pages 88–94)

1

2. Yes, he did.	**6.** Yes, he did.
3. Yes, he did.	**7.** No, she didn't.
4. No, they didn't.	**8.** No, he didn't.
5. Yes, he did.	

2

2. Did you do all the homework? Yes, I did. (OR No, I didn't.)
3. Did you take a bath this morning? Yes, I did. (OR No, I didn't.)
4. Did your best friend come over to your house last night? Yes, he / she did. (OR No, he / she didn't.)
5. Did you go to bed early last night? Yes, I did. (OR No, I didn't.)
6. Did your English teacher teach you new grammar last week? Yes, he / she did. (OR No, he / she didn't.)
7. Did you visit the United States ten years ago? Yes, I did. (OR No, I didn't.)
8. Did your mother and father get married a long time ago? Yes, they did. (OR No, they didn't.)
9. Did you watch television last night? Yes, I did. (OR No, I didn't.)

3

Answers will vary.
3. Did you buy food for dinner?
4. got
5. Did you meet Glen for lunch?
6. ate
7. Did you write a letter to Rena?
8. mailed
9. Did you go to the bank?
10. deposited
11. Did you return the book to the library?
12. took
13. Did you look for a birthday present for Jane?
14. bought
15. Did you call the doctor?
16. said
17. Did you bake some cookies?
18. had
19. Did you pick the children up at 4:00?
20. forgot

4

2.	f	**4.**	g	**6.**	a	**8.**	h
3.	b	**5.**	i	**7.**	d	**9.**	c

5

2. When did a person walk on the moon for the first time? In 1969.
3. What did William Shakespeare write? Plays like *Romeo and Juliet*.
4. Where did the Olympic Games start? In Greece.
5. Why did many people go to California in 1849? They wanted to find gold.
6. How long did Bill Clinton live in the White House? Eight years.

7. What did Alfred Hitchcock make? Movies.
8. Why did the Chinese build the Great Wall? They wanted to keep foreigners out of the country.
9. How long did World War II last in Europe? About six years.
10. When did Christopher Columbus sail to America? In 1492.

6

2.	Who gave	**7.**	Who did she send
3.	Who did you see	**8.**	Who cleaned
4.	Who called?	**9.**	Who did she marry?
5.	Who wrote	**10.**	Who did they stay
6.	Who took		

UNIT 23 (pages 95–102)

1

2.	There is	**5.**	there are	**8.**	There are
3.	there are	**6.**	There are	**9.**	There is
4.	There is	**7.**	there is	**10.**	there is

2

2. There is a computer in the store.
3. There are two restaurants on the first floor.
4. There are people at the door.
5. There is a sweater in the bag.
6. There is a bookstore between the cafés.
7. There are burgers on the menu.
8. There are boxes on the floor.
9. There are five children near the man and woman.

3

3. There is a clock for sale.
4. There is a bicycle for sale.
5. There is a bed for sale.
6. There are televisions for sale.
7. There are balls for sale.
8. There are hats for sale.
9. There are books for sale.
10. There are suitcases for sale.
11. There are shoes for sale.
12. There are lamps for sale.
13. There are CDs for sale.

4

3. There are two beds in every room.
4. There are two closets in every room.
5. There isn't a telephone in every room.
6. There is a television in every room.
7. There is an air conditioner in every room.
8. There isn't a refrigerator in every room.
9. There isn't a swimming pool at the hotel.
10. There are two restaurants at the hotel.

11. There are four tennis courts at the hotel.
12. There aren't tourist shops at the hotel.
13. There are two parking lots at the hotel.

5

3. There are two banks. They are on Main Street.
4. There are three clothing stores. They aren't very expensive.
5. There aren't any bookstores.
6. There are four drugstores. They're small.
7. There are three gas stations. They are in the center of town.
8. There aren't any hospitals.
9. There aren't any movie theaters.
10. There are two restaurants. They are open for lunch and dinner.
11. There are three schools. They aren't far from Main Street.
12. There are two supermarkets. They are big.
13. There aren't any swimming pools.

6

2. Yes, there are.
3. No, there aren't.
4. Yes, there are.
5. Yes, there are.
6. No, there aren't.
7. No, there aren't.
8. No, there aren't.
9. Yes, there are.

7

2. Are there many elephants in India? Yes, there are.
3. Is there a desert in Canada? No, there isn't.
4. Are there camels in Saudi Arabia? Yes, there are.
5. Is there a long river in the Sahara Desert? No, there isn't.
6. Are there many lions in Russia? No, there aren't.
7. Are there mountains in Kenya? Yes, there are.
8. Are there many people in Antarctica? No, there aren't.
9. Is there a big city in Thailand? Yes, there is.
10. Is there a monkey in your garden? No, there isn't.

8

2. there
3. It's
4. There's
5. there
6. there's
7. It's
8. There are
9. They're
10. they're
11. There's
12. She's

UNIT 24 (pages 103–108)

1

2. some chocolate
3. two paragraphs
4. your e-mail
5. the coffee
6. the door

2

2. you
3. him
4. it
5. her
6. them
7. us
8. me

3

1. me
2. you
3. his
4. she, her
5. its, it
6. we, us
7. their, them

4

2. us
3. them
4. you
5. her
6. you
7. her
8. them
9. us
10. him
11. them
12. him

5

2. She loves him.
3. They love us.
4. We love them.
5. Tell me the answer.
6. Show her the paper.
7. Take them some flowers.
8. Send me a postcard.

6

2. It, it
3. she, her
4. him, He
5. I, me
6. they, them
7. we, us
8. you

7

2. e
3. g
4. h
5. c
6. b
7. a
8. d

8

2. answers, you
3. this letter, Korea
4. this joke, Bill
5. the salt and pepper, me
6. the story, me
7. your passport, me
8. the information, you

9

2. He gave Bob a CD.
3. He gave his brother a video game.
4. He gave Marge some earrings.
6. He gave a book to Bill.
7. He gave some sunglasses to his cousin.
8. He gave a ring to his girlfriend.

10

2. it to them
3. them to her
4. them to him
5. it to her
6. them to me

11

2. I lent some money to him.
3. The man is showing something to the women.
4. She always gives them some help.
5. Did you tell him the answer?

6. I send all my friends birthday cards.
7. Throw the ball to me.
8. You didn't explain this sentence to us.
9. He owes me fifty dollars.

UNIT 25 (pages 109–114)

1

2. 5	**6.** 8	**10.** 4	**14.** 8
3. 7	**7.** 4	**11.** 5	**15.** 3
4. 1	**8.** 1	**12.** 7	
5. 9	**9.** 8	**13.** 2	

2

Count Nouns—eggs, vegetables, napkins, bags, potato chips, toothbrushes
Non-count Nouns—ice cream, fruit, milk, rice, food, bread, fish

3

Count Nouns—a student, some teeth, some children, some friends, an animal, some people, an uncle, a television, some questions, a computer
Non-count Nouns—some water, some paper, some homework, some advice, some traffic, some furniture, some money, some information, some rain, some oil

4

2. a	**5.** a	**8.** b	**10.** a
3. a	**6.** a	**9.** b	**11.** b
4. a	**7.** a		

5

2. a	**5.** a	**7.** the, The
3. the	**6.** the, a	**8.** a, a
4. the		

6

3. He bought some orange juice.
4. He didn't buy any lemons.
5. He bought a newspaper.
6. He didn't buy any bread.
7. He didn't buy any onions.
8. He didn't buy a toothbrush.
9. He bought some potatoes.
10. He didn't buy any lettuce.
11. He didn't buy any carrots.
12. He bought some butter.
13. He bought some milk.
14. He bought some eggs.

7

Answers will vary.
a lot of / any—food in my refrigerator, money in my pocket, books next to my bed, shirts in my closet, friends, free time, children, work to do today, questions for my teacher, jewelry, medicine in my bathroom, problems with English grammar, photographs in my wallet, ice cream at home
a little / much—cheese in my pocket, food in my refrigerator, money in my pocket, free time, work to do today, jewelry, medicine in my bathroom, ice cream at home
a few / many—books next to my bed, shirts in my closet, friends, children, questions for my teacher, problems with English grammar, photographs in my wallet

UNIT 26 (pages 115–120)

1

Answers will vary.

2

3. I rarely practice in the middle of the night.
4. I seldom fight with customers.
5. I often drive at night.
6. I am always careful.
7. I almost always find the problem with the car.
8. I never put lemon in milk.
9. I am bored once in a while
10. The hospital is open every day.
11. I almost never wear a suit and tie to work.
12. We are frequently away from home for three or four days at a time.

3

2. How often does Donna play basketball? She frequently plays basketball.
3. How often does David swim? He never swims.
4. How often do Barbara and Ed play basketball? They never play basketball.
5. How often does Ed jog? He often jogs.
6. How often does Barbara swim? She swims three times a week.
7. How often do Barbara and David jog? They rarely jog.
8. How often do Ed and George swim? They swim once or twice a week.
9. How often do George and David play basketball? They play basketball almost every day.
10. How often does George jog? He almost never jogs.
11. How often do you jog?
12. How often do you do exercises?

4

2. a	**5.** c	**8.** h	**11.** j
3. b	**6.** f	**9.** l	**12.** g
4. e	**7.** k	**10.** d	

5

2. drives, is (OR 's) driving a bus
3. fixes cars, is (OR 's) fixing cars
4. serves food, is (OR 's) serving food
5. paint pictures, are (OR 're) painting pictures
6. do experiments, are (OR 're) doing experiments
7. write articles, are (OR 're) writing articles
8. cuts meat, is (OR 's) cutting meat
9. counts money, is (OR 's) counting money
10. bake bread and cake, are (OR 're) baking bread and cake
11. waters plants and flowers, is (OR 's) watering plants and flowers
12. feeds animals, is (OR 's) feeding animals

6

2. Are you doing
3. am cutting
4. Do you prepare
5. eat
6. do you have
7. eat
8. go
9. are getting
10. doesn't go
11. Do your kids go
12. don't stay up
13. get up
14. are
15. does your daughter do
16. Does she watch
17. practices
18. is practicing
19. does she practice
20. Does she play
21. are
22. am working
23. is
24. Do you have

UNIT 27 (pages 121–124)

1

3. have, non-action verb
4. have, action verb
5. know, non-action verb
6. are . . . packing, action verb
7. need, non-action verb
8. 'm writing, action verb
9. Does . . . rain, action verb
10. Do . . . send, action verb
11. looks, non-action verb
12. looks, action verb
13. owe, non-action verb
14. visit, action verb

2

2. a
3. b
4. a
5. a
6. b
7. a
8. b
9. a
10. a
11. a
12. b
13. b
14. a

3

2. don't care
3. Do you want
4. is playing
5. don't know
6. don't have
7. is raining
8. have
9. don't have
10. don't need
11. like
12. wants
13. don't think
14. has
15. is doing
16. hear
17. is talking
18. is talking
19. doesn't understand
20. is getting
21. do you know
22. know
23. don't know

UNIT 28 (pages 124–125)

1

2. g
3. f
4. i
5. b
6. c
7. a
8. e
9. d

2

2. Terry hates traveling (OR to travel).
3. Marsha loves taking (OR to take) photographs.
4. Elena loves writing (OR to write) poems.
5. Steve enjoys being on an airplane.
6. Dana enjoys speaking other languages.
7. Rena hates to work (OR working) in an office.
8. Leo enjoys learning new things.

3

2. to swim (OR swimming)
3. to help
4. to talk
5. to move
6. to be
7. to receive (OR receiving)
8. to study (OR studying)
9. to relax
10. studying

UNIT 29 (pages 126–132)

1

2. made
3. left
4. were
5. didn't have
6. didn't play
7. bought
8. didn't eat
9. watched

2

2. No, they weren't. (OR Yes, they were.)
3. Yes, I did. (OR No, I didn't.)
4. Yes, he was. (OR No, he wasn't.)
5. Yes, it was. (OR No, it wasn't.)
6. Yes, I did. (OR No, I didn't.)
7. Yes, I was. (OR No, I wasn't.)
8. No, they didn't. (OR Yes, they did.)
9. Yes, we did. (OR No, we didn't.)
10. Yes, it was. (OR No, it wasn't.)
11. Yes, he / she did. (OR No, he / she didn't.)
12. Yes, I was. (OR No, I wasn't.)

3

2. Were you good at history in school? Yes, it was my favorite subject.
3. Were your history books interesting? They were okay.
4. Were you a talkative child? No, I was very quiet.
5. Were your parents born in the United States? No, they were born in Colombia.
6. Was your mother born in 1942? Yes, she was born in May 1942.
7. Was Michael Jordan a great baseball player? No, he was a great basketball player.
8. Was the movie about Ray Charles good? Yes, the actor was outstanding.

4

2. b	5. a	8. b
3. a	6. a	9. b
4. b	7. b	10. a

5

2. was, h	6. did, c	10. did, f
3. did, i	7. was, a	11. did, j
4. was, b	8. was, l	12. was, d
5. did, g	9. were, k	

6

2. were you
3. was it
4. were they afraid
5. was the score
6. was the name of the store
7. were they born
8. were they here
9. were you with (OR was with you)
10. was Eleanor Roosevelt

UNIT 30 (pages 133–141)

1

2. Karen and her boyfriend, Tom, are going to have dinner at a Mexican restaurant this evening.
3. Karen is going to graduate next month.
4. Karen's mother is going to visit tomorrow evening.
5. Karen and her roommate are going to move next week.
6. Karen is going to see the dentist this afternoon.
7. Karen is going to check her e-mail tonight.

2

2. Max is going to leave the office in 15 minutes.
3. Max and Debbie are going to get married in six months.
4. Debbie is going to start a new job in two weeks.
5. Debbie is going to take Max to her parents' home in four days.

3

Answers will vary.

4

Possible answers
I am (OR am not) going to study.
I am (OR am not) going to go shopping.
I am (OR am not) going to take pictures.
I am (OR am not) going to watch TV.
I am (OR am not) going to go out with friends.
I am (OR am not) going to listen to music.
I am (OR am not) going to visit relatives.
I am (OR am not) going to talk on the telephone.
I am (OR am not) going to take a shower.
I am (OR am not) going to check my e-mail.
I am (OR am not) going to go skiing.
I am (OR am not) going to stay home.

5

Possible answers
2. She's going to drive.
3. They're going to take a trip.
4. They're going to take pictures.
5. He's going to watch a movie.
6. He's going to study.

6

2. She isn't going to take
3. She isn't going to take
4. They aren't going to play
5. They aren't going to watch
6. I'm not going to eat
7. We aren't going to swim
8. He isn't going to see
9. I'm not going to wake up
10. He isn't going to deliver

7

2. Who is going to cook tonight?
3. When is dinner going to be ready?
4. Why is he going to cook so much food?
5. How long is he going to need to cook the dinner?
6. Who is going to come?
7. How is he going to cook the lamb?

8. Where are all of your guests going to sit?
9. What are you going to do?
10. How long are your guests going to stay?

8

2. What is he going to make?
3. Why is he going to cook so much food?
4. How is he going to cook the lamb?
5. Who is going to come?
6. How long is he going to need to cook the dinner?
7. What are you going to do?
8. When is dinner going to be ready?
9. How long are your guests going to stay?
10. Where are all of your guests going to sit?

9

3. 'm doing, now
4. 're having, future
5. 're moving, future
6. Are having, now
7. Are leaving, future
8. are sleeping, now
9. are going, future
10. is coming, now

10

2. They are flying to London at 7:30 on May 8.
3. They are arriving in London at 6:45 A.M. on May 9.
4. They are staying at the London Regency Hotel on May 9 and 10.
5. They are visiting Buckingham Palace at 2:00 P.M. on May 9.
6. They are having tea at the Ritz Hotel at 4:30 on May 9.
7. They are going to the theater at 7:30 on May 9.
8. They are going on a tour of central London at 9:00 A.M. on May 10.
9. They are eating lunch at a typical English pub at 12:00 P.M. on May 10.
10. They are leaving for Scotland at 8:00 A.M. on May 11.

11

2. Are you going shopping this weekend? Yes, I am. (OR No, I'm not.)
3. Are you working next week? Yes, I am. (OR No, I'm not.)
4. Is your friend having a party next Saturday? Yes, he / she is. (OR No, he / she isn't.)
5. Are your classmates studying with you tonight? Yes, they are. (OR No, they aren't.)
6. Is your neighbor coming to your place tomorrow? Yes, she is. (OR No, she isn't.)
7. Are your parents moving next year? Yes, they are. (OR No, they aren't.)

8. Are your classmates having dinner together tomorrow? Yes, they are. (OR No, they aren't.)
9. Are you and your friends playing video games on the weekend? Yes, we are. (OR No, we aren't.)
10. Is your teacher making lunch for you tomorrow? Yes, he / she is. (OR No, he / she isn't.)

12

2. When are you leaving?
3. How are you getting there? (OR How are you going?)
4. Why are you driving?
5. How long are you staying?
6. Who are you going with?
7. What are you taking?

UNIT 31 (pages 142–146)

1

2. I'll get you some water.
3. I'll help you.
4. I'll buy you some.
5. I'll turn on the air conditioner.
6. I'll make you a sandwich.
7. I'll get you some aspirin.
8. I'll drive you.
9. I'll wash them.

2

2. He'll be very happy there.
3. I'll be there early.
4. She won't do it.
5. It'll be hot tomorrow.
6. They won't come.
7. You won't get the job.

3

| 2. a | 4. a | 6. b | 8. a |
| 3. b | 5. a | 7. b | 9. b |

4

2. I won't leave late.
3. It won't be hot (OR warm).
4. Coffee won't cost more.
5. The dishes won't be dirty.
6. We won't come before seven o'clock.
7. Mr. and Mrs. McNamara won't buy a new car.
8. I won't make many eggs.
9. Valerie won't lose the game.
10. The parking lot won't be full.

5

2. Will I be		11. won't be	
3. will marry		12. will bother	
4. will I meet		13. won't like	
5. will be		14. Will our home have	
6. Will she love		15. won't leave	
7. will we meet		16. won't bother	
8. won't have		17. will become	
9. will be		18. Will that make	
10. will I be			

6

2. took		9. don't sit	
3. was		10. don't lie	
4. ate		11. 'll be	
5. wasn't		12. 'll return	
6. are resting		13. won't be	
7. aren't sitting		14. 'll be	
8. aren't lying			

UNIT 32 (pages 147–150)

1

Answers will vary.

2

2. They may (OR might) listen to the weather report.
3. He may (OR might) not drive in the snow.
4. They may (OR might) stay home.
5. She may (OR might) go to the beach.
6. We may (OR might) not ride our bikes in the hot weather.
7. You may (OR might) need a hat.
8. I may (OR might) not like the weather there.
9. The weather report may (OR might) be wrong.
10. The weather may (OR might) improve.

3

3. may	5. will	7. may	9. will
4. will	6. may	8. will	10. may

4

3. may (OR might) have an accident.
4. may (OR might) break.
5. may (OR might) not win.
6. may (OR might) get lost.
7. may (OR might) not live.
8. may (OR might) bite.
9. may (OR might) get sick.
10. may (OR might) close.

UNIT 33 (pages 151–155)

1

2. d	5. g	8. e	11. j
3. a	6. h	9. l	12. i
4. c	7. f	10. k	

2

3. One carton.	7. Four (rolls).
4. Two heads.	8. Three bars.
5. Three (bottles).	9. One tube.
6. One (box).	10. Two (jars).

3

4. Is there a cell phone in your pocket? Yes, there is. (OR No, there isn't.)
5. Is there any money in your wallet? Yes, there is. (OR No, there isn't.)
6. Are there any CDs in your bedroom? Yes, there are. (OR No, there aren't.)
7. Are there any flowers in your kitchen? Yes, there are. (OR No, there aren't.)
8. Are there any cars on your street? Yes, there are. (OR No, there aren't.)
9. Is there a computer in your bedroom? Yes, there is. (OR No, there isn't.)
10. Is there a DVD player in your home? Yes, there is. (OR No, there isn't.)
11. Is there a remote control next to your bed? Yes, there is. (OR No, there isn't.)
12. Is there any jewelry in your home? Yes, there is. (OR No, there isn't.)
13. Is there any food on your kitchen table? Yes, there is. (OR No, there isn't.)
14. Is there any furniture in your living room? Yes, there is. (OR No, there isn't.)

4

3. How much flour do you need?
4. How much sugar do you have?
5. How many bananas do you want?
6. How many oranges do you want?
7. How much cereal do you need?
8. How many potatoes do you need?
9. How much milk do you want?
10. How many roses do you want?
11. How many cookies do you have?
12. How much money do you have?

5

2. That is (OR is not) enough exercise.
3. That is (OR is not) enough fruit.
4. That is (OR is not) enough spinach.
5. That is (OR is not) enough water.
6. That is (OR is not) enough sleep.

UNIT 34 (pages 156–160)

1

2. too crowded
3. too old
4. too hot
5. too heavy

6. too expensive
7. too big
8. too young

2

2. There are too many days.
3. There are too many numbers.
4. There is too much water.
5. There is too much furniture.
6. There is too much food.
7. There are too many birds.
8. There is too much shampoo.
9. There are not enough batteries.
10. There is not enough toothpaste.
11. There is not enough air.
12. There are not enough chairs.

3

3. There were too few people for two teams.
4. We had too little paper for everyone in the class.
5. There was too little food for 15 people.
6. You have too little information.
7. There are too few bedrooms in that apartment.
8. We had too little time for that test.
9. There are too few bananas for a banana cake.
10. There are too few sales clerks at that store.

4

2. b   5. a   8. a
3. a   6. b   9. b
4. b   7. b   10. a

UNIT 35 (pages 161–164)

1

3. correct
4. correct
5. Please bring me my car.
6. Where is her car?
7. correct
8. correct
9. We need our car.
10. Their car is expensive.
11. correct
12. Why do you want your car?

2

2. Mine   5. Yours   8. hers
3. his   6. theirs   9. Theirs
4. ours   7. his   10. ours

3

2. my, yours, mine   5. Their, their, theirs
3. hers, hers   6. his, his
4. our, ours

4

2. Our, We, us   6. your, Yours, You
3. We, ours, our   7. It, it, Its
4. me, my, I   8. their, theirs, them
5. His, his, him   9. her, She, hers

UNIT 36 (pages 165–167)

1

2. b   5. a   7. a
3. b   6. b   8. a
4. b

2

2. I pay by credit card   5. I sit here
3. I come in   6. I bring my boyfriend
4. I speak to the doctor

3

2. Can I (OR May I) open the window?
3. Can I (OR May I) use the telephone?
4. Can I (OR May I) get a ride (with you)?
5. Can I (OR May I) use (OR borrow) your eraser?
6. Can I (OR May I) have a drink of water?
7. Can I (OR May I) ask you a question?
8. Can I (OR May I) sit at the empty table in the corner?

UNIT 37 (pages 168–172)

1

1. At the bus station.   3. At a movie theater.
2. On an airplane.

2

3. The teacher would like to see you.
4. Would the children like hamburgers or hot dogs?
5. Would you like to check your e-mail on my computer?
6. Would Paul like to come to the party?
7. My husband would like rice with his fish.
8. Neil and Jane would like a bigger apartment.
9. Would you like to have a cup of coffee with me?
10. We would like to go home now.

3

2. Would you like
3. Would you like
4. would like / 'd like
5. Would you like
6. What would you like to do
7. Where would you like to go
8. Would you like to go
9. Would you like to see
10. What time would you like to go
11. would like to get / 'd like to get
12. Where would you like to eat

4

2. Would (OR Could) you (please) give me the key to my room?
3. Would (OR Could) you (please) explain the meaning of the word *grateful*?
4. Would (OR Could) you (please) give me change for a dollar?
5. Would (OR Could) you (please) take a picture of me and my friends?
6. Would (OR Could) you (please) take me to the airport?
7. Would (OR Could) you (please) help me with my suitcases?
8. Would (OR Could) you (please) show me the brown shoes in the window?
9. Would (OR Could) you (please) sit down?

5

2. a   4. b   6. a
3. a   5. a

UNIT 38 (pages 173–177)

1

2. shouldn't   5. shouldn't   8. shouldn't
3. should   6. should   9. should
4. shouldn't   7. should   10. shouldn't

2

2. I ought to look up information about the country on the Internet.
3. Business people ought to learn about the customs of other countries.
4. The visitor ought to bring a gift.
5. We ought to be careful.

3

2. I should learn how to speak the language.
3. Ms. Jones should put her e-mail address on her business card.
4. You should plan your trip carefully.
5. The students should ask more questions.

4

2. should look for another one
3. shouldn't smoke
4. should go to the dentist
5. should wash it
6. shouldn't leave a tip
7. should study more
8. should leave early
9. shouldn't watch it
10. shouldn't touch it

5

2. Why should we have
3. How many (people) should we invite?
4. Who should we invite?
5. What should we buy?
6. What should we cook?
7. Where should we get
8. What should we do?
9. When should we send

6

2. a   5. a   8. e
3. e   6. c   9. d
4. d   7. b   10. b

7

2. had better not serve shrimp
3. had better get a couple of bottles
4. had better not let the dog in the house
5. had better ask Costas to bring her
6. had better not sit together at the table
7. had better invite him
8. had better rent a video
9. had better borrow some from the neighbors

UNIT 39 (pages 178–184)

1

Answers will vary.

2

2. have to, don't have to
3. don't have to, have to
4. have to, don't have to
5. don't have to, have to
6. have to, don't have to
7. don't have to, have to
8. have to, don't have to
9. have to, don't have to
10. don't have to, have to

3

2. has to leave early today.
3. have to go food shopping today.

4. have to take a taxi.
5. doesn't have to work late today.
6. don't have to clean up their room.
7. has to take some medicine.
8. don't have to pay for the tickets.
9. has to wear a suit and tie this morning.
10. doesn't have to do housework.

4

2. I don't have to write everything 10 times.
3. The teacher didn't have to come early yesterday.
4. One student had to stay after class yesterday.
5. I don't have to check e-mail every day.
6. My friends didn't have to work last week.
7. The school has to have clean classrooms.
8. The teacher doesn't have to work on the weekend.
9. My classmates and I have to pay attention in class.
10. I have to write down the new words.

5

2. You must stop.
3. You mustn't turn right.
4. You mustn't turn left.
5. You mustn't drive faster than 55 mph.
6. You mustn't park in this area.
7. You mustn't make a U-turn.
8. You mustn't pass.
9. You must go more slowly.

6

2. They had to find someone to take care of their dog.
3. They had to get to the airport on time.
4. They didn't have to get up early every morning.
5. They didn't have to go to work.
6. They had to look for a hotel.
7. They didn't have to make the bed every morning.
8. They had to pack and unpack suitcases.
9. They had to pay their hotel bill.
10. They didn't have to wash dishes.

7

2. Does your mother have to get up at six o'clock in the morning? Yes, she does. (OR No, she doesn't.)
3. Did you have to cook last night? Yes, I did. (OR No, I didn't.)
4. Does your best friend have to do this exercise? Yes, he / she does. (OR No, he / she doesn't.)
5. Do you have to be in English class on time? Yes, I do. (OR No, I don't.)

6. Do your friends have to learn English? Yes, they do. (OR No, they don't.)
7. Did your father have to shave yesterday? Yes, he did. (OR No, he didn't.)
8. Did your best friend have to go to work yesterday? Yes, he / she did. (OR No, he / she didn't.)
9. Did you have to take a test last week? Yes, I did. (OR No, I didn't.)

8

2. does she have to take a test?
3. does he have to leave early?
4. did the students have to wait for their teacher?
5. did you have to meet after class?
6. does the teacher have to talk to?
7. did he have to pay for the class?
8. does she have to buy?
9. do you have to finish your paper?
10. did the schools have to close?

UNIT 40 (pages 185–187)

1

✓—2, 7

2

One Syllable—fast, high, hot, long, old, small
Two Syllables—crowded, easy, friendly, heavy, messy, noisy, pretty
Three or Four Syllables—dangerous, difficult, expensive, intelligent

3

2. better	7. more comfortable
3. farther	8. more careful
4. more intelligent	9. prettier
5. worse	10. more difficult
6. messier	11. easier

4

2. longer than	8. more crowded than
3. more expensive than	9. noisier than
4. bigger than	10. heavier than
5. higher than	11. faster than
6. hotter than	12. friendlier than
7. more dangerous than	

5

Answers to the questions will vary.
3. Is this book cheaper or more expensive than your notebook?
4. Is your country bigger or smaller than Canada?
5. Is your English pronunciation better or worse than last year?

6. Which is more interesting, romantic movies or war movies?
7. Which is healthier, coffee or tea?
8. Which is nicer, dinner at home or dinner in a restaurant?

UNIT 41 (pages 188–190)

1

3. adverb   7. adverb   11. adverb
4. adjective 8. adjective 12. adjective
5. adverb   9. adjective
6. adverb   10. adverb

2

3

2. quietly   7. badly
3. dangerously   8. fast
4. angrily   9. patiently
5. happily   10. easily
6. well

4

2. good, good   6. careful, carefully
3. fast, fast   7. easy, easily
4. tired, tired   8. bad, badly
5. angry, angrily   9. serious, seriously

UNIT 42 (pages 191–198)

1

2. h   4. a   6. f   8. d
3. g   5. b   7. e

2

2. The questions are too difficult to answer.
3. The shirt is too small to wear.
4. It is too hot (OR warm) outside to go running.
5. The store is too far to walk.
6. The soup is too cold to eat.

3

2. The story wasn't interesting enough.
3. Your room isn't neat enough.

4. Your hair isn't short enough.
5. You aren't old enough to watch that kind of TV program.
6. The numbers aren't big enough to see.

4

2. too   4. very   6. too   8. very
3. too   5. very   7. very   9. too

5

2. That cell phone is too expensive to buy.
3. I'm too tired to wait.
4. The steak was too tough (for Sandra) to eat.
5. Jeffrey isn't old enough to drive.
6. They aren't good enough to play on the team.
7. The tea is too hot to drink.
8. She's smart enough to do the work.

6

3. too frightened   8. too short
4. not big enough   9. not safe enough
5. too late   10. warm enough
6. hot enough   11. not sunny enough
7. too tight

7

✓—2, 3, 4, 6, 7

8

3. as   6. than   9. as   11. than
4. than   7. as   10. than   12. than
5. as   8. as

9

4. Trains aren't as fast as airplanes.
5. January is as cold as February.
6. The chair is as comfortable as the sofa.
7. The governor of Oregon isn't as famous as the president of the United States.
8. The bank isn't as far as the post office.
9. Limes are as sour as lemons.
10. Jazz is more relaxing than rock music.
11. Chocolate ice cream isn't as good as vanilla ice cream.
12. Some people are more violent than other people.
13. College isn't as easy as high school.
14. These boxes are as heavy as those boxes.

10

2. Are you the same height as your brother?
3. Is your mother the same age as your father?
4. Is the dining room the same size as the living room?
5. Are the apples the same price as the oranges?

6. Are you the same weight as your brother?
7. Is *War and Peace* the same length as *Crime and Punishment*?
8. Is the subway station the same distance as the bus stop?

11

3. A bike is the same as a bicycle.
4. A TV is the same as a television.
5. North America is different from the United States.
6. 10,362 is different from 10.362.
7. 3×16 is the same as 16×3.
8. $16 \div 3$ is different from $3 \div 16$.
9. $1 is different from £1.
10. A snack bar is different from a restaurant.
11. 12:00 P.M. is the same as noon.
12. A plane is the same as an airplane.

UNIT 43 (pages 199–202)

1

2. Shanghai Garden
3. The Big Oven
4. Donnelly's
5. Circo
6. Circo
7. The Big Oven

2

2. the worst
3. the hardest
4. the most beautiful
5. the busiest
6. the funniest
7. the best
8. the ugliest
9. the most popular
10. the lowest
11. the fastest
12. the most charming

3

Answers will vary.
2. What is one of the tallest buildings in the world?
3. What is one of the most crowded cities in the world?
4. What is one of the most famous buildings in the world?
5. What is one of the most polluted places in the world?
6. Who is one of the best athletes in the world?

4

Answers for part b of each question will vary.
2. a. A teenager is the oldest of the three.
   b. A child is older than a baby.
3. a. Nigeria is the hottest of the three.
   b. Spain is hotter than Sweden.
4. a. A highway is the widest of the three.
   b. A street is wider than a path.
5. a. A city is the biggest of the three.
   b. A town is bigger than a village.
6. a. An elephant is the heaviest of the three.
   b. A gorilla is heavier than a fox.
7. a. An hour is the longest of the three.
   b. A minute is longer than a second.
8. a. Boxing is the most dangerous of the three.
   b. Soccer is more dangerous than golf.

Test: Units 1–3

PART ONE

DIRECTIONS: *Circle the letter of the correct answer to complete each sentence.*

Example:

Li _____ from China.   A B Ⓒ D

(A) am   (C) is
(B) are   (D) not

1. **A:** Are you a doctor?   A B C D
   B: Yes, _____.

   (A) I'm   (C) am
   (B) I am   (D) I'm not

2. My friends and I _____ baseball fans.   A B C D

   (A) are   (C) is
   (B) am   (D) not

3. _____ at home last night.   A B C D

   (A) They were   (C) They are
   (B) I were   (D) We was

4. _____ very tired yesterday.   A B C D

   (A) I were   (C) I wasn't
   (B) I were not   (D) Was I

5. Ping-Pong _____ a great game.   A B C D

   (A) is   (C) are
   (B) not   (D) am

6. Andre Agassi _____ a tennis player.   A B C D

   (A) am   (C) is
   (B) are   (D) not

7. **A:** _____ a new student?   A B C D
   B: No, she isn't.

   (A) Are she   (C) She
   (B) Is she   (D) Is

8. **A:** Are your clothes comfortable?
   B: _____ are.   A B C D

    (A) Yes, it   (C) Yes, they
    (B) No, they   (D) No, it

9. _____ in Seoul last year?   A B C D

    (A) Were she   (C) Were I
    (B) Was they   (D) Was she

10. **A:** Were they in class last week?
    B: No, they _____.   A B C D

    (A) was   (C) wasn't
    (B) were   (D) weren't

11. You _____ at the park yesterday.   A B C D

    (A) was   (C) wasn't
    (B) were   (D) aren't

12. Halle Berry is an actor. _____ a tennis player.   A B C D

    (A) He not   (C) She not
    (B) She's not   (D) Isn't

PART TWO

Directions: Each sentence has four underlined words or phrases. The four underlined parts of the sentence are marked A, B, C, and D. Circle the letter of the one underlined word or phrase that is NOT CORRECT.

Example:

Li and Ping <u>am</u> <u>from</u> <u>a city in</u> <u>China</u>.   Ⓐ B C D
        A   B   C   D

13. <u>Was</u> Mike and Rita <u>at</u> <u>the party</u> <u>last night</u>?   A B C D
   A   B   C   D

14. <u>My friends</u> and I <u>am</u> <u>not</u> <u>famous</u>.   A B C D
    A   B C   D

15. We <u>are</u> <u>late</u> <u>for class</u> <u>today?</u>   A B C D
     A   B   C   D

16. The *Star Wars* movies <u>it</u> <u>are</u> <u>not</u> <u>comedies</u>.   A B C D
              A B C   D

17. <u>It</u> <u>was</u> <u>yesterday</u> <u>cloudy</u>.   A B C D
   A B   C   D

18. <u>Are</u> <u>Ken and Nancy</u> they <u>good</u> <u>soccer players</u>?   A B C D
   A   B   C   D

19. <u>Are</u> <u>Toronto and Vancouver</u> <u>city</u> <u>in</u> Canada?   A B C D
   A   B   C D

20. Were <u>two weeks ago</u> <u>you</u> <u>and Henry</u> <u>in Mexico</u>?   A B C D
       A   B   C   D

Test: Units 4–7

PART ONE

Directions: Circle the letter of the correct answer to complete the sentence.

Example:

I am _____.   Ⓐ B C D

  (**A**) a teacher   (**C**) teacher
  (**B**) an teacher   (**D**) teachers

1. **A:** _____ is *Pride and Prejudice*?   A B C D
   B: It's a famous book.

  (**A**) What   (**C**) Why
  (**B**) Who   (**D**) Where

2. Sonal is _____.   A B C D

  (**A**) from india   (**C**) from India
  (**B**) India   (**D**) an India

3. They are _____.   A B C D

  (**A**) nice photo   (**C**) a nice photo
  (**B**) photos nice   (**D**) nice photos

4. **A:** _____ is the Louvre?   A B C D
   B: It's in Paris, France.

  (**A**) Who   (**C**) Where
  (**B**) Why   (**D**) Who

5. Lisa is _____.   A B C D

  (**A**) a artist   (**C**) artist
  (**B**) an artist   (**D**) artists

6. The book is _____ the table.   A B C D

  (**A**) on   (**C**) at
  (**B**) in   (**D**) between

7. _____ are on a business trip.   A B C D

  (**A**) The man   (**C**) The men
  (**B**) A man   (**D**) The mans

8. **A:** Why is the store closed?

   B: _____

   (A) New York.   (C) It's closed.
   (B) Because it's Sunday. (D) It's a toy store.

   A B C D

9. She's _____ woman.

   (A) old   (C) olds
   (B) a old   (D) an old

   A B C D

10. I'm _____ work right now.

    (A) in   (C) at
    (B) on   (D) under

    A B C D

11. The flowers are _____.

    (A) beautifuls   (C) a beautiful
    (B) beautiful   (D) an beautiful

    A B C D

12. Your watch is _____ the newspaper and the glasses.

    (A) at   (C) on the corner of
    (B) in   (D) between

    A B C D

PART TWO

DIRECTIONS: Each sentence has four underlined words or phrases. The four underlined parts of the sentence are marked A, B, C, and D. Circle the letter of the <u>one</u> underlined word or phrase that is NOT CORRECT.

Example:

<u>My</u> <u>tooth</u> are <u>very white</u> and <u>clean</u>.
  A   B   C   D

A Ⓑ C D

13. <u>She</u> is <u>engineer</u> <u>from</u> <u>Russia</u>.
    A   B   C   D

A B C D

14. <u>The</u> <u>apartment</u> <u>is</u> <u>on</u> 10 Maple Street.
    A   B   C   D

A B C D

15. <u>Were</u> <u>the days</u> <u>sunny</u> and <u>hots</u>?
    A   B   C   D

A B C D

16. <u>My</u> <u>pant</u> <u>are</u> <u>cheap</u>.
    A   B   C   D

A B C D

17. <u>The bakery</u> <u>is</u> <u>next</u> the <u>restaurant</u>.
    A   B   C   D

A B C D

18. <u>Who</u> <u>are</u> <u>the artist</u> and <u>the photographer</u> from?
    A   B   C   D

A B C D

19. <u>We</u> <u>were</u> at <u>interesting</u> <u>market</u> yesterday.
    A   B   C   D

A B C D

20. <u>Is</u> <u>what</u> <u>the name</u> of <u>that</u> <u>book</u>?
    A   B   C   C   D

A B C D

Test: Units 8–10

PART ONE

DIRECTIONS: Circle the letter of the correct answer to complete the sentence.

Example:

Ted _____ at the mall.   A Ⓑ C D

(A) work   (C) do not work
(B) works   (D) do work

1. I _____ to bed at ten every night.   A B C D

   (A) goes   (C) don't go
   (B) doesn't go   (D) don't goes

2. _____ wants a new car.   A B C D

   (A) You   (C) They
   (B) We   (D) He

3. She doesn't have a dog or _____.   A B C D

   (A) a cat   (C) have a cat
   (B) doesn't have a cat   (D) not a cat

4. We _____ the laundry every Friday.   A B C D

   (A) does   (C) does do
   (B) do   (D) don't

5. **A:** Do you live in Tokyo?   A B C D
   B: Yes, I _____.

   (A) lives   (C) live
   (B) does   (D) do

6. **A:** _____ a lot?   A B C D
   B: Yes, he does.

   (A) Studies he   (C) Does he study
   (B) He studies   (D) Do he study

7. **A:** Do you like your roommate?   A B C D
   B: No, I _____.

   (A) do   (C) doesn't
   (B) don't   (D) does

8. **A:** Do they have library cards?　　　　　　　　　　　　A　B　C　D
   B: Yes, _____.

   (A) they has　　　　　　　(C) they do
   (B) they do have　　　　　(D) they does

9. **A:** What do they drink?　　　　　　　　　　　　　　A　B　C　D
   B: _____.

   (A) Drink coffee　　　　　(C) They drinks coffee
   (B) They drink coffee　　(D) He drinks coffee

10. **A:** _____ do you feel?　　　　　　　　　　　　　A　B　C　D
    B: Sad.

    (A) How　　　　　　　　(C) Whom
    (B) Why　　　　　　　　(D) When

11. **A:** _____ Tara play soccer with?　　　　　　　　A　B　C　D
    B: Janet.

    (A) When do　　　　　　(C) Why does
    (B) Who(m) does　　　　(D) What do

12. **A:** _____ you get up?　　　　　　　　　　　　　A　B　C　D
    B: At eight o'clock in the morning.

    (A) When　　　　　　　(C) When do
    (B) Where　　　　　　　(D) When does

PART TWO

DIRECTIONS: Each sentence has four underlined words or phrases. The four underlined parts of the sentence are marked A, B, C, and D. Circle the letter of the <u>one</u> underlined word or phrase that is NOT CORRECT.

Example:

Lucy, <u>you</u> <u>looks</u> very <u>beautiful</u> <u>today</u>.　　　　　A　Ⓑ　C　D
　　　　A　　B　　　　　C　　　　D

13. She <u>likes</u> apples, but <u>she</u> <u>not</u> <u>like</u> oranges.　　　A　B　C　D
　　　　A　　　　　　　B　　C　　D

14. We <u>doesn't</u> <u>buy</u> new <u>shoes</u> <u>every weekend</u>.　　　A　B　C　D
　　　　A　　　B　　　　C　　　D

15. <u>Does</u> <u>is</u> <u>he</u> <u>from</u> California?　　　　　　　　A　B　C　D
　　A　　B　C　　D

16. <u>Does</u> <u>she</u> <u>has</u> <u>a</u> good CD player?　　　　　　A　B　C　D
　　A　　　B　　C　D

17. <u>Does</u> I <u>need</u> <u>new</u> <u>clothes</u>?　　　　　　　　　A　B　C　D
　　A　　　　B　　C　　D

18. <u>Who</u> <u>does</u> watches <u>TV</u> <u>on the weekends</u>?　　A　B　C　D
　　A　　B　　　　　　C　　　D

19. <u>Why</u> <u>helps</u> Jackie <u>at</u> <u>home</u>?　　　　　　　A　B　C　D
　　A　　B　　　　　C　D

20. <u>What</u> <u>do</u> you <u>dreams</u> <u>about</u> at night?　　　A　B　C　D
　　A　　B　　　　C　　　D

Test: Units 11–14

PART ONE

DIRECTIONS: Circle the letter of the correct answer to complete the sentence.

Example:

_____ time does the movie start?   Ⓐ B C D

(A) What   (C) Why
(B) When   (D) Where

1. A: Where's that CD?   A B C D
   B: _____ in my bedroom.

   (A) It's   (C) Its
   (B) That's   (D) It

2. A: _____ is the party?   A B C D
   B: It's on Saturday.

   (A) What time   (C) When day
   (B) What day   (D) When time

3. A: _____ pens are these?   A B C D
   B: They're Leo's.

   (A) Who's   (C) Whose
   (B) Who   (D) Whom

4. A: What time does class start?   A B C D
   B: _____ nine o'clock in the morning.

   (A) In   (C) It
   (B) On   (D) At

5. Children play a lot of video games _____ days.   A B C D

   (A) those   (C) that
   (B) this   (D) these

6. A: Do you have a bike?   A B C D
   B: Yes, I _____.

   (A) have a   (C) have ones
   (B) have one   (D) have this one

7. A: What _____ your birthday?   A B C D
   B: It's September 8.

   (A) is   (C) is day
   (B) day is   (D) day

8. **A:** Whose T-shirt is this?
   B: _____.   A B C D

   (A) Its Annas   (C) It's Anna's
   (B) It's Anna   (D) Its Anna's

9. _____ car is very expensive.   A B C D

   (A) Mike's   (C) Mikes
   (B) Mike   (D) Mikes'

10. _____ pants are red.   A B C D

   (A) This   (C) That
   (B) These   (D) That's

11. **A:** Does she like these?   A B C D
    B: No, she likes _____.

   (A) those   (C) ones
   (B) those ones   (D) one

12. _____ flowers in the store window are really beautiful.   A B C D

   (A) Those   (C) This
   (B) These   (D) That

PART TWO

DIRECTIONS: Each sentence has four underlined words or phrases. The four underlined parts of the sentence are marked A, B, C, and D. Circle the letter of the <u>one</u> underlined word or phrase that is NOT CORRECT.

Example:

The conference <u>starts</u> <u>on</u> 8:30 <u>in</u> <u>the morning</u>.   A Ⓑ C D
           A   B   C   D

13. <u>The</u> red shoes <u>are</u> cheap, and <u>the white</u> <u>one</u> are expensive.   A B C D
    A   B   C   D

14. <u>Is</u> <u>Miami</u> <u>in</u> New York <u>and</u> Florida?   A B C D
   A   B   C   D

15. I live <u>on</u> <u>Forty-five</u> Street <u>on</u> the <u>third</u> floor.   A B C D
      A   B   C   D

16. We <u>need</u> three <u>skirts</u>, two black <u>one</u> and a gray <u>one</u>.   A B C D
     A   B   C   D

17. New Year's Day <u>is</u> <u>on</u> the <u>one</u> <u>day</u> of the year.   A B C D
            A B   C D

18. <u>That's</u> <u>party</u> last night <u>was</u> <u>great</u>.   A B C D
    A   B   C D

19. <u>Your</u> <u>notebook</u> <u>is</u> in <u>your's</u> bag.   A B C D
    A   B   C   D

20. <u>My</u> <u>aunt's</u> <u>names</u> <u>are</u> Meg and Fiona.   A B C D
    A   B   C   D

Test: Units 15–19

PART ONE

DIRECTIONS: Circle the letter of the correct answer to complete the sentence.

Example:

She _____ right now.   A (B) C D

(A) resting   (C) is rests
(B) is resting   (D) are resting

1. A: Let's play soccer.   A B C D
   B: I can't. _____ play with George instead?

(A) Let's   (C) Why don't you
(B) Let's not   (D) Why don't we

2. A: Let's have hamburgers for lunch.   A B C D
   B: Sorry, not today. _____ have pizza instead.

(A) Why we don't   (C) Let's
(B) Why don't   (D) Let's not

3. A: Are you playing tennis right now?   A B C D
   B: No, _____.

(A) I'm not   (C) I not
(B) you're not   (D) I am

4. The car _____ $20,000.   A B C D

(A) cost   (C) costing
(B) is costing   (D) costs

5. A: Can they play the guitar?   A B C D
   B: No, _____.

(A) they can   (C) they could
(B) they can't   (D) they couldn't

6. _____ watching TV at the moment.   A B C D

(A) We're   (C) We
(B) Are   (D) We is

7. I _____ speak French three years ago.   A B C D

(A) can   (C) couldn't
(B) can't   (D) cannot

8. Don't _____ late! A B C D

    (A) is   (C) are
    (B) be   (D) to be

9. **A:** Is she going to the movies? A B C D
   B: Yes, _____.

    (A) she's   (C) she's going
    (B) she is   (D) she going

10. _____ the train to work today. A B C D

    (A) Don't   (C) Don't take
    (B) Not take   (D) Take not

11. _____ there. A B C D

    (A) Please to sit   (C) To sit please
    (B) Sit please   (D) Please sit

12. **A:** Could you drive last year? A B C D
   B: Yes, _____.

    (A) I can   (C) I can't
    (B) I could   (D) I couldn't

13. **A:** Why don't we go to the pool? A B C D
   B: _____. The water is too cold.

    (A) OK   (C) Sounds good to me
    (B) Good idea   (D) No, I don't feel like it

14. Nowadays a lot of people _____ English. A B C D

    (A) learns   (C) are learning
    (B) is learning   (D) are learn

15. **A:** _____ are they doing? A B C D
   B: They're shopping.

    (A) What   (C) Where
    (B) Why   (D) Who

PART TWO

DIRECTIONS: Each sentence has four underlined words or phrases. The four underlined parts of the sentence are marked A, B, C, and D. Circle the letter of the <u>one</u> underlined word or phrase that is NOT CORRECT.

Example:

They <u>are</u> <u>work</u> <u>at home</u> <u>today</u>.   A Ⓑ C D
    A   B   C   D

16. <u>My</u> cell phone <u>aren't</u> <u>working</u> <u>right now</u>.   A B C D
    A   B   C   D

17. <u>Let's</u> <u>not</u> <u>us</u> <u>go</u> to the party too early.   A B C D
    A   B   C D

18. <u>Do</u> <u>doing</u> <u>your</u> homework, <u>please</u>.   A B C D
    A   B   C   D

19. <u>You could</u> <u>cook</u> <u>when</u> you <u>were</u> 10 years old? A B C D
       A   B   C   D

20. Who <u>is</u> <u>it</u> <u>having</u> spaghetti for <u>lunch</u>?   A B C D
       A B C   D

21. <u>Please</u> <u>to</u> <u>walk</u> five blocks and <u>turn</u> left.   A B C D
    A   B   C   D

22. We <u>cannot</u> <u>run</u> fast <u>20 years</u> <u>ago</u>.   A B C D
      A   B   C   D

23. <u>Where</u> <u>he is</u> <u>living</u> <u>these days</u>?   A B C D
    A   B   C   D

24. <u>Why</u> <u>not</u> <u>you</u> buy some <u>souvenirs?</u>   A B C D
    A   B   C   D

25. I <u>am</u> <u>driving</u> and <u>am</u> <u>listening</u> to music.   A B C D
    A   B   C   D

Test: Units 20–22

PART ONE

Directions: Circle the letter of the correct answer to complete the sentence.

Example:

We _____ Shanghai last year.   A B Ⓒ D

(A) visit   (C) visited
(B) are visiting   (D) visits

1. **A:** Did you read that book?   A B C D
   B: Yes, _____.

   (A) I read   (C) I did read
   (B) I did   (D) did read

2. They didn't fly to London _____.   A B C D

   (A) last week ago   (C) week ago
   (B) last week   (D) last ago

3. I _____ a lot for the Spanish test.   A B C D

   (A) studyd   (C) studied
   (B) studyed   (D) studyied

4. **A:** _____ did you leave early last night?   A B C D
   B: Because I was tired.

   (A) When   (C) Who
   (B) Where   (D) Why

5. **A:** _____ yesterday morning?   A B C D
   B: Mieko.

   (A) Whom called   (C) Who called
   (B) Who did call   (D) What called

6. They _____ at the conference last week.   A B C D

   (A) wasn't   (C) didn't be
   (B) was   (D) weren't

7. You didn't _____ a new car.   A B C D

   (A) buy   (C) buyed
   (B) bought   (D) brought

8. She _____ to my birthday party.   A B C D

    (**A**) come   (**C**) didn't came

    (**B**) came   (**D**) did came

9. He _____ to the movies last night.   A B C D

    (**A**) doesn't go   (**C**) didn't go

    (**B**) did go not   (**D**) didn't goes

10. **A:** Did they visit Brazil last year?   A B C D

    B: _____ didn't.

    (**A**) No, they   (**C**) No,

    (**B**) Yes, they   (**D**) They

11. Pablo and Livia _____ to work this morning.   A B C D

    (**A**) walked   (**C**) walk

    (**B**) walking   (**D**) walkied

12. My children _____ in Stockholm, Sweden.   A B C D

    (**A**) born   (**C**) were born

    (**B**) was born   (**D**) were borned

PART TWO

Directions: Each sentence has four underlined words or phrases. The four underlined parts of the sentence are marked A, B, C, and D. Circle the letter of the <u>one</u> underlined word or phrase that is NOT CORRECT.

Example:

You <u>watches</u> <u>the news</u> <u>yesterday</u> <u>morning</u>.   Ⓐ B C D
      A   B   C   D

13. <u>I</u> <u>did</u> <u>not</u> <u>saw</u> that movie two weeks ago.   A B C D
   A   B   C D

14. <u>They</u> <u>bought</u> a friend <u>to the party</u> <u>last night</u>.   A B C D
   A   B   C   D

15. She <u>two weeks ago</u> <u>had</u> <u>dinner</u> <u>with a friend</u>.   A B C D
       A   B   C   D

16. <u>Where</u> <u>you did</u> <u>live</u> <u>five years ago</u>?   A B C D
    A   B   C   D

17. <u>Why</u> <u>did</u> <u>she</u> <u>went</u> to the park?   A B C D
   A   B   C D

18. <u>It</u> <u>snowed</u> in Chicago <u>last week</u> <u>ago</u>.   A B C D
   A B   C   D

19. <u>What</u> <u>did</u> <u>happened</u> in Paris <u>last week</u>?   A B C D
    A   B   C   D

20. <u>We</u> was <u>not</u> <u>at that restaurant</u> <u>yesterday</u>.   A B C D
   A   B   C   D

Test: Units 23–25

PART ONE

DIRECTIONS: Circle the letter of the correct answer to complete the sentence.

Example:

_____ two women at the door.   A B Ⓒ D

(A) There's   (C) There are
(B) There is   (D) They are

1. A: _____ did you sell?   A B C D
   B: My TV.

   (A) To whom   (C) What
   (B) Who   (D) To what

2. I gave _____.   A B C D

   (A) a gift him   (C) to him a gift
   (B) gift   (D) him a gift

3. _____ nice restaurant on Main Street.   A B C D

   (A) There a   (C) There's
   (B) There's a   (D) There are

4. _____ any twins in my family.   A B C D

   (A) There isn't   (C) There are
   (B) There's   (D) There aren't

5. We didn't drink _____.   A B C D

   (A) some coffee   (C) many coffee
   (B) any coffee   (D) a few coffee

6. Oscar and I are teachers, and _____ teach at Huxtable School.   A B C D

   (A) we   (C) he
   (B) they   (D) us

7. The guests ate _____.   A B C D

   (A) a little peanuts   (C) a few peanuts
   (B) little peanuts   (D) much peanut

8. _____ e-mail Chuck every day.   A B C D

   (A) I and Bob   (C) Bob and me
   (B) Bob and I   (D) Me and Bob

9. There's _____ in this food.   A B C D

   (A) a lot of salt   (C) many salts
   (B) a few salt   (D) one salt

10. I bought an apple and two oranges. _____ apple was good,   A B C D
    but I didn't like the oranges.

   (A) The   (C) A
   (B) An   (D) —

11. _____ a mall near here?   A B C D

   (A) Is there any   (C) Are there
   (B) Is there   (D) There is

12. There are two dogs in the yard, and _____ big.   A B C D

   (A) there are   (C) they are
   (B) they   (D) there are

PART TWO

Directions: Each sentence has four underlined words or phrases. The four underlined parts of the sentence are marked A, B, C, and D. Circle the letter of the <u>one</u> underlined word or phrase that is NOT CORRECT.

Example:

<u>There are</u> <u>any</u> <u>good shows</u> on TV <u>right now</u>?   Ⓐ B C D
   A   B   C   D

13. <u>I</u> <u>owe</u> a lot of <u>money</u> to <u>they</u>.   A B C D
  A B   C   D

14. <u>You</u> and Joan <u>showed</u> <u>the</u> photos <u>her</u>.   A B C D
  A   B   C   D

15. <u>The</u> <u>baby</u> <u>drinks</u> <u>much</u> milk.   A B C D
  A   B   C   D

16. <u>There</u> are <u>any</u> <u>mountains</u> <u>in</u> Florida.   A B C D
  A   B   C   D

17. We <u>sent</u> it <u>the letters</u> <u>to</u> <u>them</u>.   A B C D
      A   B   C D

18. <u>You</u> <u>did</u> <u>use</u> any <u>pepper</u> in the recipe.   A B C D
  A   B   C   D

19. <u>I</u> <u>cooked</u> three <u>chicken</u> for the <u>party</u>.   A B C D
  A   B   C   D

20. I like Miami <u>because</u> <u>there</u> <u>are</u> beaches <u>their</u>.   A B C D
          A   B   C   D

Test: Units 26–29

PART ONE

DIRECTIONS: Circle the letter of the correct answer to complete the sentence.

Example:

We _____ at six o'clock every morning.

(A) get up   (C) are getting up
(B) gets up   (D) getting up

Ⓐ B C D

1. He _____ his car a couple of hours ago.

(A) finished to fix   (C) finish fixed
(B) finished fixing   (D) finish to fixed

A B C D

2. How often _____ to the movies?

(A) are you going   (C) do you go
(B) go you   (D) you go

A B C D

3. Children _____ toys.

(A) are loving   (C) love
(B) loves   (D) is loving

A B C D

4. It usually _____ in England.

(A) is raining   (C) rains
(B) rain   (D) are raining

A B C D

5. Are you _____ a new job?

(A) trying to find   (C) trying finding
(B) try finding   (D) trying find

A B C D

6. I _____ on my computer right now.

(A) are working   (C) am working
(B) work   (D) works

A B C D

7. She _____ soccer yesterday.

(A) did not play   (C) not played
(B) does not play   (D) played not

A B C D

8. My parents _____ golf.

(A) don't hate   (C) hate not
(B) are not hating   (D) not hating

A B C D

9. He _____ tennis.   A B C D

   (A) plays sometimes   (C) play sometimes
   (B) sometimes play   (D) sometimes plays

10. Those bikes _____ to me.   A B C D

    (A) belong   (C) belongs
    (B) is belonging   (D) are belonging

11. We _____ a DVD player.   A B C D

    (A) want buying   (C) want to buying
    (B) want buy   (D) want to buy

12. We _____ about the homework right now.   A B C D

    (A) are thinking   (C) is thinking
    (B) think   (D) thinks

13. They plan _____ on their vacation in Hawaii.   A B C D

    (A) surfing   (C) surf
    (B) to surf   (D) to surfing

14. A: Was it hot yesterday?   A B C D
    B: No, it _____.

    (A) was   (C) wasn't
    (B) isn't   (D) not was

15. A: _____ born in Mexico?   A B C D
    B: Yes, I was.

    (A) Was I   (C) Are you
    (B) Were you   (D) You were

PART TWO

DIRECTIONS: Each sentence has four underlined words or phrases. The four underlined parts of the sentence are marked A, B, C, and D. Circle the letter of the <u>one</u> underlined word or phrase that is NOT CORRECT.

Example:

<u>Do</u> <u>they</u> <u>running</u> <u>in the park</u> right now?   Ⓐ B C D
 A   B   C   D

16. Grandpa <u>is</u> <u>being</u> <u>happy</u> <u>today</u>.   A B C D
            A   B   C   D

17. <u>How often</u> <u>do</u> <u>you</u> <u>going</u> to concerts?   A B C D
     A   B   C   D

18. <u>We</u> <u>agreed</u> <u>to</u> <u>having</u> pizza for dinner.   A B C D
     A   B   C   D

19. <u>Where</u> <u>were</u> you <u>buy</u> that <u>dress</u>?   A B C D
     A   B   C   D

20. <u>You</u> <u>are</u> <u>know</u> <u>him</u> very well.   A   B   C   D
       A   B   C   D

21. <u>They</u> <u>avoid</u> <u>to drive</u> late <u>at night</u>.   A   B   C   D
       A   B   C   D

22. <u>When</u> <u>did</u> <u>you</u> <u>getting</u> up this morning?   A   B   C   D
       A   B   C   D

23. I <u>hate</u> <u>to play</u> soccer, but I <u>enjoy</u> <u>to watch</u> it.   A   B   C   D
        A   B   C   D

24. <u>Always</u> I <u>am</u> <u>late</u> for <u>English class</u>.   A   B   C   D
       A   B   C   D

25. I <u>think</u> <u>he</u> <u>is having</u> very short <u>hair</u>.   A   B   C   D
       A   B   C   D

TEST: UNITS 30–32

PART ONE

DIRECTIONS: Circle the letter of the correct answer to complete the sentence.

Example:

They _____ eat at a restaurant tomorrow night.   A B Ⓒ D

(A) going to   (C) are going to
(B) are going   (D) going to

1. Some people say cars _____ in the future.   A B C D

(A) are flying   (C) will fly
(B) going to fly   (D) is flying

2. **A:** Remember to close the windows!   A B C D
   B: Don't worry. I _____ forget.

(A) won't   (C) might
(B) may   (D) 'll

3. He is _____ a vacation this summer.   A B C D

(A) going take   (C) take
(B) going to take   (D) will take

4. **A:** _____ are you coming home tonight?   A B C D
   B: At 10 o'clock.

(A) Why   (C) What
(B) Who   (D) When

5. **A:** The phone is ringing.   A B C D
   B: _____ it.

(A) I'm answering   (C) Will I answer
(B) I'll answer   (D) I'll answering

6. _____ some juice at the store.   A B C D

(A) Will I buy   (C) I buy
(B) I'll buy   (D) I'll

7. **A:** When will she get a dog?   A B C D
   B: She _____ a dog. She'll get a cat.

(A) will   (C) won't get
(B) won't   (D) not will get

8. **A:** How old is your son?
   B: He _____ 14 this year.

    (A) will be   (C) may be
    (B) will   (D) may

A   B   C   D

9. Mrs. Baxter _____ to buy a new car this year.

    (A) isn't going   (C) isn't
    (B) isn't go   (D) is going not

A   B   C   D

10. **A:** _____ going to have a party this weekend?
    B: My best friend.

    (A) Who are   (C) Is who
    (B) Who   (D) Who's

A   B   C   D

11. Be careful with that glass. You _____ it.

    (A) might   (C) break
    (B) may not   (D) might break

A   B   C   D

12. **A:** Where can I buy some milk?
    B: I'm not sure. That store _____ have some.

    (A) maybe   (C) will
    (B) may   (D) 'll

A   B   C   D

PART TWO

DIRECTIONS: Each sentence has four underlined words or phrases. The four underlined parts of the sentence are marked A, B, C, and D. Circle the letter of the <u>one</u> underlined word or phrase that is NOT CORRECT.

Example:

We <u>are</u> <u>going</u> to <u>watch</u> a movie <u>in</u> 3:00.
   A   B   C   D

A   B   C   Ⓓ

13. <u>We'll</u> <u>being</u> <u>late</u> for the party <u>tonight</u>.
    A   B   C   D

A   B   C   D

14. I <u>think</u> it <u>maybe</u> <u>be</u> <u>sunny</u> tomorrow.
   A   B   C   D

A   B   C   D

15. <u>Are</u> your friend <u>moving</u> <u>to</u> Boston <u>next year</u>?
   A   B   C   D

A   B   C   D

16. <u>It</u> <u>won't</u> <u>raining</u> tomorrow <u>afternoon</u>.
   A   B   C   D

A   B   C   D

17. <u>Will</u> <u>I'll</u> <u>have</u> many <u>children</u>?
   A   B   C   D

A   B   C   D

18. Jack <u>might</u> <u>not</u> <u>be</u> <u>win</u> the race.
        A   B C D

A   B   C   D

19. Why <u>is</u> <u>he</u> <u>going</u> <u>calling</u> his mother now?
    A B   C   D

A   B   C   D

20. We <u>are</u> <u>not</u> <u>go</u> <u>to</u> the theater tonight.
    A   B C D

A   B   C   D

TEST: UNITS 33–35

PART ONE

DIRECTIONS: Circle the letter of the correct answer to complete the sentence.

Example:

I'm going to buy _____ gum.   Ⓐ B C D

(A) a pack of   (C) a head of
(B) a loaf of   (D) a can of

1. That's _____ daughter.   A B C D

(A) they   (C) their
(B) them   (D) theirs

2. **A:** There are four people at the party, and we have 15 boxes of cookies!   A B C D
   B: Oh, no. We have _____ food.

(A) too many   (C) too much
(B) not enough   (D) much

3. **A:** I love our new car.   A B C D
   B: Well, we don't like _____. It's too small.

(A) our   (C) we
(B) your   (D) ours

4. **A:** Is that your jacket?   A B C D
   B: No. _____ is green.

(A) My   (C) Mine jacket
(B) Mine   (D) Yours

5. **A:** _____ of soda did he buy?   A B C D
   B: Two bottles.

(A) How much bottles   (C) How many bottles
(B) How many   (D) How much

6. **A:** How much soap do you need?   A B C D
   B: _____.

(A) Two bars.   (C) Two heads.
(B) Two cans.   (D) Two rolls.

7. Are there _____ chairs in your living room?   A B C D

(A) a   (C) much
(B) an   (D) any

8. **A:** These shoes are size 10. Do you want them?   A B C D
   B: No. I wear size 8. They're _____.

   (A) too big   (C) too small
   (B) big too   (D) small too

9. **A:** There's only one bathroom in that house.   A B C D
   B: That's _____ bathrooms. We need two.

   (A) too little   (C) enough
   (B) too few   (D) too many

10. **A:** This red cell phone is Ted's.   A B C D
    B: No, it isn't. The blue one is _____.

    (A) his   (C) he
    (B) him   (D) Ted

11. _____ new tube of toothpaste in the bathroom.   A B C D

    (A) There's some   (C) There are some
    (B) There's a   (D) There's any

12. **A:** There's too little ice cream at this party.   A B C D
    B: I know. There's _____ ice cream for everyone.

    (A) too few   (C) not enough
    (B) little   (D) enough

PART TWO

DIRECTIONS: Each sentence has four underlined words or phrases. The four underlined parts of the sentence are marked A, B, C, and D. Circle the letter of the <u>one</u> underlined word or phrase that is NOT CORRECT.

Example:

<u>How</u> <u>much</u> <u>boxes</u> of cereal <u>do</u> we need?   A Ⓑ C D
  A   B   C   D

13. The hat is <u>my</u>, but the <u>pen</u> <u>is</u> <u>hers</u>.   A B C D
        A   B C D

14. <u>How</u> <u>many</u> <u>CD</u> do you <u>have</u>?   A B C D
  A   B   C   D

15. I <u>don't</u> <u>have</u> <u>money enough</u> for <u>this</u> TV.   A B C D
    A   B   C   D

16. <u>There</u> <u>are</u> <u>too</u> <u>little</u> cheese on this pizza.   A B C D
    A   B C D

17. <u>There</u> <u>are</u> <u>too</u> <u>much</u> people at this store.   A B C D
    A   B C D

18. <u>Is</u> that <u>yours</u> cat <u>in</u> the yard?   A B C D
  A   B   C   D

19. One <u>meal</u> a day <u>is</u> <u>no</u> <u>enough</u> food.   A B C D
       A   B C D

20. <u>Is</u> <u>there</u> <u>an</u> computer on <u>your</u> desk?   A B C D
  A   B   C   D

TEST: UNITS 36–39

PART ONE

DIRECTIONS: Circle the letter of the correct answer to complete the sentence.

Example:

_____ smoke in here. It's against the law.   A Ⓑ C D

(A) You can   (C) You may
(B) You can't   (D) May you

1. _____ your cell phone?   A B C D

(A) May I use   (C) I may not use
(B) I may use   (D) May use

2. A: _____ get up early?   A B C D
   B: Yes, I do. I have to get up at 5 a.m.

(A) Did you have   (C) Do you have to
(B) Do have to   (D) Did you have to

3. A: How much _____ pay for their vacation last year?   A B C D
   B: Five hundred dollars.

(A) did they have to   (C) did they have
(B) do they have to   (D) they did have to

4. A: I'm cold.   A B C D
   B: _____ put on a coat.

(A) You better   (C) You'd better
(B) Should you   (D) You'd should

5. Tennis players _____ know how to type.   A B C D

(A) not have to   (C) don't have
(B) don't have to   (D) have not to

6. A: _____ to come to my party?   A B C D
   B: Yes, I would.

(A) Would like   (C) Would you like
(B) You'd like   (D) Would you

7. _____ to buy three tickets for the movie.   A B C D

(A) We'd like   (C) We'd
(B) We like   (D) Would we like

8. People _____ near babies.   A B C D

   (A) ought to not   (C) ought smoke
   (B) shouldn't smoke   (D) should smoke not

9. A: I can't speak Spanish, but I'm moving to Mexico soon.   A B C D
   B: You_____ Spanish classes.

   (A) should take   (C) take should
   (B) shouldn't take   (D) ought take

10. A: _____ we pick up Aniko at the airport?   A B C D
    B: At 7 o'clock.

    (A) Who should   (C) Where should
    (B) Why should   (D) When should

11. A: Is Maria going to buy a TV?   A B C D
    B: No, she _____ buy a TV. Her mother gave her a TV.

    (A) don't have to   (C) doesn't has to
    (B) has to   (D) doesn't have to

12. A: _____ a drink of water?   A B C D
    B: Sure.

    (A) May have   (C) Can I have
    (B) Can I   (D) I may have

13. A: May I stay out until midnight tonight?   A B C D
    B: No, you _____!

    (A) may   (C) may I
    (B) can   (D) may not

14. You _____ cook tonight. I'll bring home a pizza.   A B C D

    (A) doesn't have to   (C) has to
    (B) have to   (D) don't have to

15. A: Would you like a cookie?   A B C D
    B: _____.

    (A) No, I would.   (C) No, I don't.
    (B) Yes, thank you.   (D) Yes, I would like.

PART TWO

DIRECTIONS: Each sentence has four underlined words or phrases. The four underlined parts of the sentence are marked A, B, C, and D. Circle the letter of the <u>one</u> underlined word or phrase that is NOT CORRECT.

Example:

<u>Could</u> <u>you</u> <u>open</u> <u>please</u> the window?
  A   B   C   D

A B C Ⓓ

16. <u>You</u> <u>mustn't</u> <u>stop</u> at <u>a</u> red light.
     A   B   C   D

A B C D

17. <u>Can</u> <u>I</u> <u>drive</u> me to the airport, <u>please</u>?
     A B   C   D

A B C D

18. <u>How</u> <u>many</u> <u>cans of soda</u> <u>we should</u> buy?
     A   B   C   D

A B C D

19. <u>Why</u> <u>does</u> we <u>have to go</u> to bed now?
     A   B   C   D

A B C D

20. <u>What time</u> <u>you would</u> <u>like</u> to <u>come</u> over?
     A   B   C   D

A B C D

21. We <u>had</u> <u>not better</u> <u>take</u> a <u>bus</u> to school.
       A   B   C   D

A B C D

22. <u>Why</u> <u>did</u> <u>they</u> <u>have</u> leave class early?
     A   B   C   D

A B C D

23. <u>Can</u> <u>I</u> <u>speaking</u> to Jackie, <u>please</u>?
     A B   C   D

A B C D

24. No, <u>you</u> <u>may</u> <u>no</u> <u>eat</u> 10 pieces of cake.
       A   B C D

A B C D

25. He <u>does</u> not <u>has to</u> <u>wear</u> a <u>suit</u> to work.
      A   B   C   D

A B C D

TEST: UNITS 40–43

PART ONE

DIRECTIONS: Circle the letter of the correct answer to complete the sentence.

Example:

Dogs are _____ cats.   Ⓐ B C D

(A) bigger than   (C) big than
(B) more big than   (D) more big

1. That bicycle is _____ this one.   A B C D

  (A) expensive than   (C) more expensive than
  (B) more expensive   (D) expensiver

2. **A:** Let's go to Benny's Bookstore.   A B C D
  B: No! It's _____ bookstore in town!

  (A) worst   (C) the best
  (B) best   (D) the worst

3. Snails move very _____.   A B C D

  (A) slow   (C) more slow
  (B) slowly   (D) fastly

4. That dress looks _____ on her.   A B C D

  (A) well   (C) good
  (B) badly   (D) goodly

5. **A:** Do you want to play football?   A B C D
  B: No, it's _____.

  (A) enough hot   (C) hot enough
  (B) too hot   (D) too hot enough

6. These shoes are _____ wear.   A B C D

  (A) too small to   (C) too small enough to
  (B) to small too   (D) small enough

7. **A:** Which is better, the big computer or the small one?   A B C D
  B: The small one is too slow. It's _____ the big one.

  (A) better than   (C) worse
  (B) worse than   (D) badder than

8. Mount Everest is _____ Mount St. Helens.　　　　A　B　C　D

(A) higher than　　　　(C) tall than
(B) high than　　　　　(D) lower than

9. A: Do you like this restaurant?　　　　　　　　　A　B　C　D
B: Yes, but it's _____ expensive.

(A) enough　　　　(C) too
(B) not enough　　(D) too very

10. A tree is _____ a flower.　　　　　　　　　　A　B　C　D

(A) different from　　(C) as the same as
(B) the same as　　　(D) different as

11. The Pacific is _____ ocean in the world.　　　　A　B　C　D

(A) biggest　　　　(C) the big
(B) the biggest　　(D) the most big

12. A: Can I play soccer with Mikey?　　　　　　　　A　B　C　D
B: No, he's _____ to play. He's only two.

(A) too old　　(C) not old
(B) very old　(D) not old enough

13. Antarctica is _____ places in the world.　　　　A　B　C　D

(A) one of the coldest　　(C) one of the most could
(B) one of coldest　　　　(D) of the coldest

14. The girl did her homework _____.　　　　　　　A　B　C　D

(A) quiet　　(C) good
(B) noisy　　(D) quietly

15. Grandma is very _____ today.　　　　　　　　　A　B　C　D

(A) tired　　(C) seriously
(B) tiredly　(D) happily

PART TWO

DIRECTIONS: Each sentence has four underlined words or phrases. The four underlined parts of the sentence are marked A, B, C, and D. Circle the letter of the <u>one</u> underlined word or phrase that is NOT CORRECT.

Example:

<u>12:00</u> A.M. <u>is</u> <u>the</u> <u>same</u> midnight.　　　　A　B　C　Ⓓ
　A　　　　 B　C　D

16. <u>It's</u> <u>too</u> dangerous <u>swim</u> <u>today</u>.　　　　　　A　B　C　D
　　A　 B　　　　　　 C　　D

17. <u>You</u> <u>should</u> be <u>more</u> <u>carefuller</u>.　　　　　　A　B　C　D
　　A　　B　　　　C　　　D

18. <u>Easiest</u> <u>subject</u> in <u>school</u> <u>is</u> Social Studies.   A B C D
      A   B   C D

19. <u>Who</u> <u>is</u> the <u>better</u> <u>student</u> in the class?   A B C D
     A B   C   D

20. Whales <u>are</u> <u>more</u> <u>heavier</u> <u>than</u> rabbits.   A B C D
        A   B   C   D

21. <u>Apples</u> <u>are</u> not <u>as</u> sweet <u>than</u> candy.   A B C D
     A   B   C   D

22. <u>Is</u> this CD player <u>same</u> <u>price</u> <u>as</u> that one?   A B C D
    A   B C D

23. <u>He</u> <u>speaks</u> French <u>and</u> German <u>fluent</u>.   A B C D
    A   B   C   D

24. <u>My</u> father <u>was</u> very <u>angrily</u> at <u>me</u>.   A B C D
    A   B   C   D

25. <u>She</u> is <u>the</u> <u>beautifullest</u> actress in <u>the</u> world.   A B C D
    A   B   C   D

Answer Key for Tests

Correct responses for Part Two questions appear in parentheses.

UNITS 1–3

Part One

1. B	4. C	7. B	10. D
2. A	5. A	8. C	11. B
3. A	6. C	9. D	12. B

Part Two

13. A (were)
14. B (are)
15. D (.)
16. A (are)

17. C (cloudy yesterday)
18. B (delete)
19. C (cities)
20. A (in Mexico two weeks ago)

UNITS 4–7

Part One

1. A	4. C	7. C	10. C
2. C	5. B	8. B	11. B
3. D	6. A	9. D	12. D

Part Two

13. B (an engineer)
14. D (at)
15. D (hot)
16. B (pants)

17. C (next to)
18. A (Where)
19. C (an interesting)
20. A (What is)

UNITS 8–10

Part One

1. C	4. B	7. B	10. A
2. D	5. D	8. C	11. B
3. A	6. C	9. B	12. C

Part Two

13. C (doesn't)
14. A (don't)
15. A (delete)
16. C (have)

17. A (Do)
18. B (delete)
19. A (Who)
20. C (dream about)

UNITS 11–14

Part One

1. A	4. D	7. B	10. B
2. B	5. D	8. C	11. A
3. C	6. B	9. A	12. A

Part Two

13. D (ones)
14. D (or)
15. B (Forty-fifth)
16. C (ones)

17. C (first)
18. A (That)
19. D (your)
20. B (aunts')

UNITS 15–19

Part One

1. C	5. B	9. B	13. D
2. C	6. A	10. C	14. C
3. A	7. C	11. D	15. A
4. D	8. B	12. B	

Part Two

16. B (isn't)
17. C (delete)

18. B (delete)
19. A (Could you)
20. B (delete)

21. B (delete)
22. A (could not OR couldn't)
23. B (is he)
24. B (don't)
25. C (delete)

UNITS 20–22

1. B	4. D	7. A	10. A
2. B	5. C	8. B	11. A
3. C	6. D	9. C	12. C

Part Two

13. D (see)
14. B (brought)
15. A (with a friend two weeks ago)
16. B (did you)

17. D (go)
18. D (delete)
19. B (delete)

20. A (I OR He OR She)

UNITS 23–25

Part One

1. C	4. D	7. C	10. A
2. D	5. B	8. B	11. B
3. B	6. A	9. A	12. C

Part Two

13. D (them)   17. B (delete)
14. D (to her)   18. B (didn't)
15. D (a lot of)   19. C (chickens)
16. B (a few OR some) 20. D (there)

UNITS 26–29

Part One

1. B	5. A	9. D	13. B
2. C	6. C	10. A	14. C
3. C	7. A	11. D	15. B
4. C	8. A	12. A	

Part Two

16. B (delete)   21. C (driving)
17. D (go)   22. D (get)
18. D (have)   23. D (watching)
19. B (did)   24. A (I am always late)
20. B (delete)   25. C (has)

UNITS 30–32

1. C	4. D	7. C	10. D
2. A	5. B	8. A	11. D
3. B	6. B	9. A	12. B

Part Two

13. B (be)   17. B (I)
14. B (will)   18. C (delete)
15. A (Is)   19. C (delete)
16. C (rain)   20. C (going)

UNITS 33–35

1. C	4. B	7. D	10. A
2. C	5. C	8. A	11. B
3. D	6. A	9. B	12. C

Part Two

13. A (mine)   17. D (many)
14. C (CDs)   18. C (your)
15. C (enough money) 19. C (not)
16. B (is)   20. C (a)

UNITS 36–39

Part One

1. A	5. B	9. A	13. D
2. C	6. C	10. D	14. D
3. A	7. A	11. D	15. B
4. C	8. B	12. C	

Part Two

16. B (must)   21. B (better not)
17. B (you)   22. D (delete/have to)
18. D (should we)   23. C (speak)
19. B (do)   24. C (not)
20. B (would you)   25. B (have to)

UNITS 40–43

Part One

1. C	5. B	9. C	13. A
2. D	6. A	10. A	14. D
3. B	7. B	11. B	15. A
4. C	8. A	12. D	

Part Two

16. C (to swim)   21. D (as)
17. D (careful)   22. B (the same)
18. A (The easiest)   23. D (fluently)
19. C (best)   24. C (angry)
20. B (delete)   25. C (most beautiful)